GEORGIA O'KEEFFE

WORKS ON PAPER

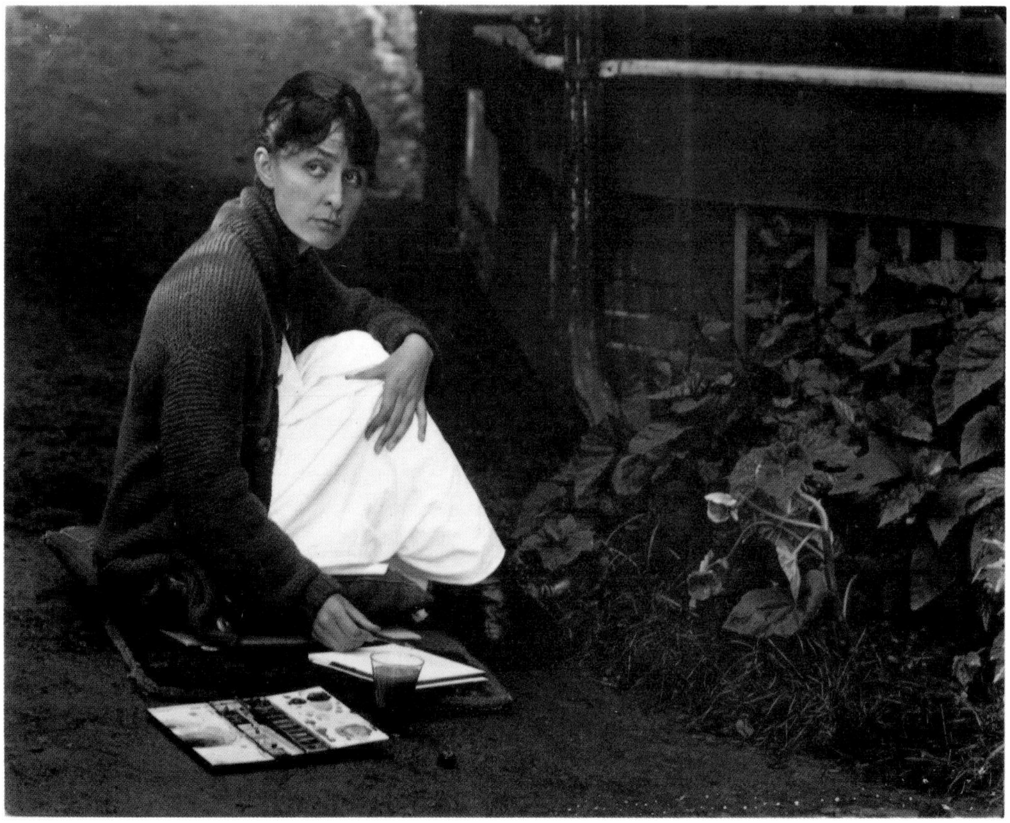

GEORGIA O'KEEFFE

Works on Paper

Introduction by David Turner
Essay by Barbara Haskell

Museum of Fine Arts
Museum of New Mexico, Santa Fe

Museum of New Mexico Press

Front Cover: *Lake George and Woods*, ca. 1922. Collection of Mr. and Mrs. John Palmer Leeper
Frontispiece: Georgia O'Keeffe, Lake George, New York, ca. 1918. Photograph by Alfred Stieglitz. Courtesy of Gilman Paper Company Collection.

PHOTO CREDITS
All photographs of works by Georgia O'Keeffe are reproduced in this publication courtesy of the owners with additional credit to the photographers of the following images: Fig. 1, Aida and Bob Mates; Figs. 2, 4, Wyatt McSpadden; Fig. 12, Helga Photo; Fig. 11, Museum of Fine Arts, boston; Plates 5, 28, Stephen R. Dolan; Plate 14, Robert Nugent; Plate 17, Malcom Varon; Plates 20, 25, Michael Jay Smith; Plate 37, Maurice Thaler.

Fifth Printing: 2001.

Manufactured in Hong Kong by Dai Nippon Printing Co., Ltd.
Typography: Business Graphics
Editing: Sarah Nestor
Design: Christopher Beisel

LIBRARY OF CONGRESS CATALOGING IN PUBLICATION DATA
O'Keeffe, Georgia, 1887-
Georgia O'Keeffe, works on paper.

Catalogue of an exhibition at the Museum of Fine Arts, Museum of New Mexico, Santa Fe, September 14–November 17, 1985.
1. O'Keeffe, Georgia, 1887- —Exhibitions.
I. Turner, David, 1948– . II. Haskell, Barbara, 1946–
III. Museum of New Mexico. Museum of Fine Arts.
IV. Title.
NC139.045A4 1985 741.973 85-5047
ISBN 0-89013-154-6
ISBN 0-89013-153-8 (pbk.)

Museum of New Mexico Press
P.O. Box 2087
Santa Fe, New Mexico 87504

CONTENTS

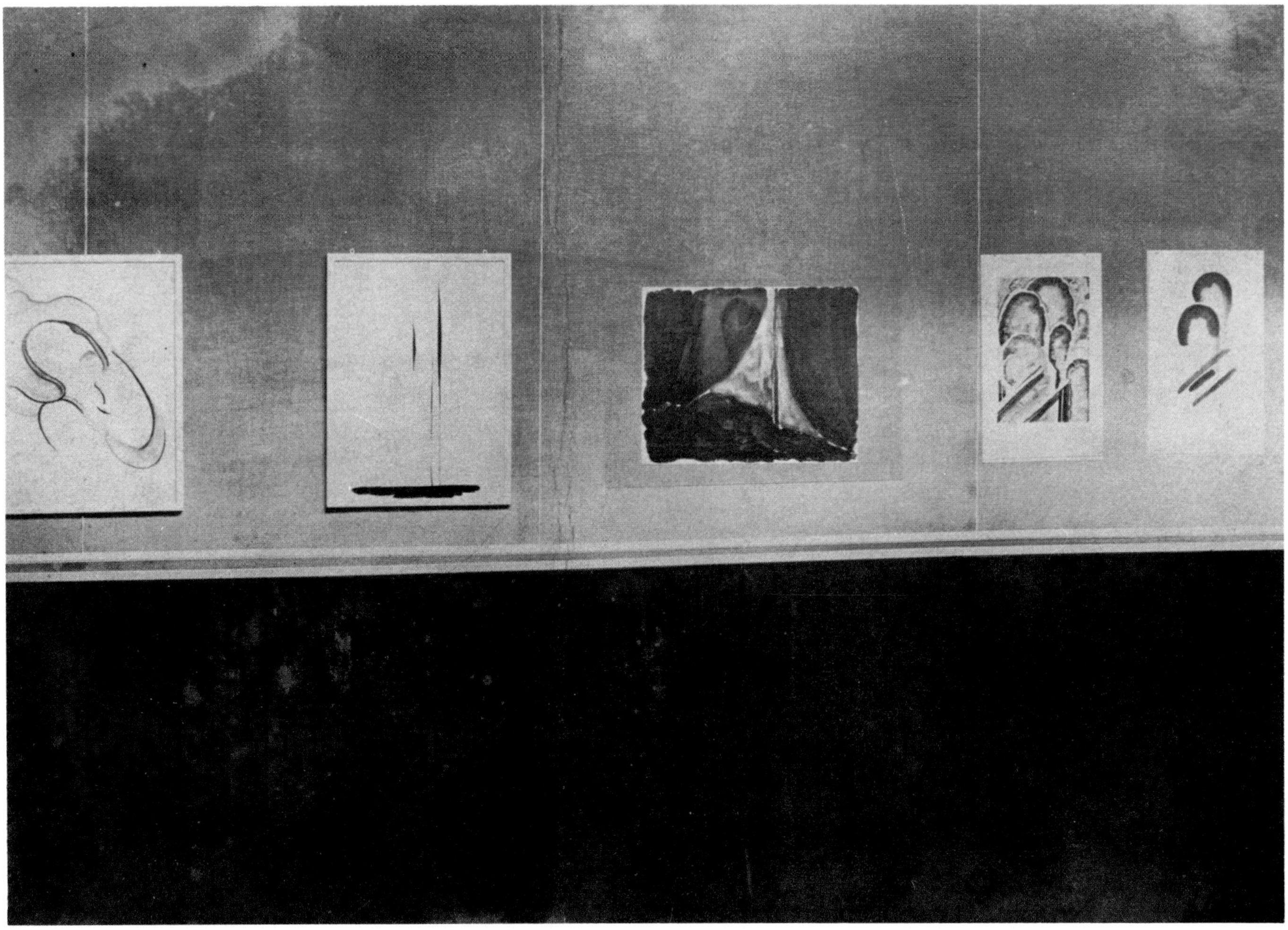

Exhibition of O'Keeffe watercolors and drawings at gallery 291, held in April-May 1917. Photograph by Alfred Stieglitz. Courtesy of Zabriskie Gallery.

INTRODUCTION

The painting of Georgia O'Keeffe possesses a singular strength that has made it one of the treasures of twentieth-century American art. During the first three decades of the century, at a time when artists could easily be informed and influenced through the museum and gallery exhibitions and reproductions in widely disseminated magazines like *Camera Work* and *American Art News*, Miss O'Keeffe developed a highly individualized, personal style in her work which she has continued to explore and refine throughout her long career. This consistency of vision, inspired by her exposure to the modernist artists who exhibited in Alfred Stieglitz' gallery 291 and demonstrated in her own regular exhibits there, led critic E. M. Benson to remark in 1936, "I never saw an O'Keeffe that reminded me of anything but O'Keeffe."

There is a story about how O'Keeffe first came to the attention of Alfred Stieglitz, who did so much to encourage her career. It involves the early charcoal drawings she made in 1915 while teaching art at Columbia College in Columbia, South Carolina. With the basic medium of sticks of charcoal on sheets of paper, O'Keeffe began to assimilate the ideas of her teacher, Arthur W. Dow, in the sensitive arrangement of lines, shapes, and space that represented personal, subjective emotions. These drawings, which were primarily abstract arrangements of forms related to nature that came from O'Keeffe's imagination, were comparable to the art by leading American modernists like Arthur Dove, John Marin, and Paul Strand. O'Keeffe sent a series of drawings to her college friend, Anita Pollitzer, for critique. When Pollitzer showed them to Alfred Stieglitz at 291 on January 1, 1916, he remarked that they were the "purest, finest, sincerest things that have entered 291 in a large while." In May of that year Stieglitz exhibited ten of those drawings at 291. This stimulation from Stieglitz led O'Keeffe to continue her work in charcoal, and later that year she began adding color to her work by using watercolor.

For three years, 1916-1918, O'Keeffe worked primarily on paper with watercolor, charcoal, and pastel. The portability of the media allowed her to walk over the West Texas plains or through the Lake George forests to paint and draw directly from nature. Yet these pictures are not purely naturalistic. Though they are based on strict observation, they reflect a free spirit which pays attention to the essential shape, form, and color in nature. The works are fresh and direct. They illustrate the immediacy of a spontaneous revelation quickly noted. They are sketches of inspired moments. O'Keeffe later turned to working more precisely in oil, but she never totally abandoned her work on paper. The later drawings and watercolors were often opportunities for her to freely explore ideas she eventually painted in oil. Or they were simply chances for her to return to the less formal, more intimately scaled media that she had previously mastered.

By assembling a group of O'Keeffe's works on paper, rarely seen together, the reader and museum visitor can begin to gain a better understanding of both the artist's process of working and the larger context of her career's output. Particularly when O'Keeffe painted watercolors in a series, like *Evening Star*, *Blue*, *Red Cannas*, and *Light Coming on the Plains*, one can watch her work on an idea that leads from subjective representation toward a greater sense of abstraction. The precious nature of the watercolors, pastels, and charcoals also requires them to be scrutinized and enjoyed in a different way than her oil paintings. The texture of the paper surface and the delicacy of the marks made by the charcoal, chalk, or water-diluted pigment make these works speak with a subtlety and familiarity. They demand the viewing attention given to a finely detailed engraving of the sixteenth century, but they also call for an openness and sensitivity to the modernist ideas of abstraction from the twentieth century.

Because of their intrinsic beauty, it has been a real pleasure for me to work on a project involving the art of Georgia O'Keeffe. I was fortunate to have taken over the plans for this present exhibition and catalogue, which were started at the Museum of Fine Arts, Santa Fe, in 1982. The project began as an attempt to recognize the many contributions Miss O'Keeffe has made to American art, particularly while living in New Mexico. Only two small exhibitions of her work have ever been held in Santa Fe: in 1975 twelve paintings were shown in the Governor's Gallery and in 1982 five paintings were exhibited at the opening dedication of the New Wing at the Museum of Fine Arts. The retrospective exhibition organized by the Amon Carter Museum showed at the University Art Museum, Albuquerque, in 1966. The plans for this exhibition were laid by Ellen Bradbury, former Director of the Museum of Fine Arts, and the initial grant proposal to the National Endowment for the Arts was prepared by Don Humphrey, curator at the Museum. When I took over the project in Fall 1983, I had a conversation with Juan Hamilton, Miss O'Keeffe's assistant. It was decided then to focus the project on her works on paper, a body of work that has never been exhibited on its own.

Loans to this exhibition were not always easy to arrange. The fragility of the paper works, particularly the pastels and charcoals, and the demand on the works to be seen in other museums and galleries made some key works unavailable. Therefore, we are extremely appreciative of those lenders who were able to let us borrow their pieces for this exhibition and reproduce them in the catalogue. For their generosity and trust, I wish to thank Mr. and Mrs. Warren Adelson, New York; Mark Carliner, Studio City, California; Steven W. Rosen and Jane Isaacs, Columbus Museum of Art, Ohio; Sid Deutsch, Sid Deutsch Gallery, New York; Carlton Overland, Elvehjem Museum of Art, Madison, Wisconsin; Maxine Rosston, The Fine Arts Museums of San Francisco, Achenbach Foundation for Graphic Arts, San Francisco, California; Kathleen Burnside, Hirschl and Adler Galleries, Inc., New York; Lawrence Fleischman and F. Frederick Bernask, Kennedy Galleries, New York; Rollin B. King, King Investments Co., Dallas, Texas; Ida Balboul and Alisa Liskin, The Metropolitan Museum of

Art, New York; Russell Bowman, Milwaukee Art Museum, Milwaukee, Wisconsin; Steven Bradley and Future Akins, The Museum, Texas Tech University, Lubbock, Texas; Andrew Robinson and Carlotta Owings, National Gallery of Art, Washington, D.C.; Mr. and Mrs. Gerald Peters, Santa Fe, New Mexico; Margaret Morris, Gerald Peters Gallery, Santa Fe, New Mexico; Dore Previn, Los Angeles, California; Stephen Goddard, The Helen Foresman Spencer Museum of Art, University of Kansas, Lawrence, Kansas; Robert L.B. Tobin, San Antonio, Texas; Emily Kass and Kevin Donovan, University Art Museum, University of New Mexico, Albuquerque, New Mexico; Joan Washburn and Gretta Meilman, Washburn Gallery, New York; Patterson Sims, Whitney Museum of American Art, New York; Richard S. Field, Yale University Art Gallery, New Haven, Connecticut; a group of anonymous lenders; and Thomas Garver, Madison Art Center, Madison, Wisconsin, and Nathaniel O. Owings, Bozeman, Montana, for helping to arrange some anonymous loans. We are also grateful to the following institutions and individuals for allowing their works to be reproduced in this catalogue: the Amarillo Art Center, Amarillo, Texas; The Arkansas Arts Center, Little Rock, Arkansas; the Art Museum, Princeton University, Princeton, New Jersey; the Beinecke Rare Book and Manuscript Library, Yale University, New Haven, Connecticut; The Brooklyn Museum, Brooklyn, New York; the Andrew Crispo Gallery, New York; Hirschl and Adler Galleries, Inc., New York; The Hirshhorn Museum and Sculpture Garden, Smithsonian Institution, Washington, D.C.; The Lane Collection, Boston, Massachusetts; Milwaukee Art Museum, Milwaukee, Wisconsin; The Museum of Modern Art, New York; the Zabriskie Gallery, New York; and Mr. and Mrs. John Palmer Leeper, San Antonio.

In the detail work of assembling the exhibition, I would like to acknowledge the help of many people including Barbara Haskell, Curator at the Whitney Museum of American Art, who wrote an insightful essay about Miss O'Keeffe's work on paper and discussed with me her thoughtful ideas about the exhibition and catalogue; Marilyn Vierra, Fine Arts Intern during the summer, 1984, who assisted in the research; Sue Critchfield, Librarian/Registrar at the Museum of Fine Arts, who helped with the loan arrangements; Claudia Gayheart and John Duran, Museum of New Mexico Registrar's office, who handled the loans and condition reports; Steve Yates, the Museum's Curator of Photography, who assembled a companion exhibition of photographic portraits of Miss O'Keeffe; Sandra Edelman, Sucha Cardoza, and Patrick Ranker, Museum of New Mexico Foundation, who helped handle the financial records; Christopher Beisel, Museum of New Mexico Exhibitions Unit, who carefully designed the handsome exhibition installation and catalogue; Jim Mafchir and Sarah Nestor, Museum of New Mexico Press, who coordinated the publication of this catalogue; Lorraine Cook and Theresa Arellano, secretaries at the Museum of Fine Arts, who typed so much material for the exhibition and catalogue; and former Museum of New Mexico Director Jean Weber, Interim Director George Ewing, and Deputy Director James R. Pahl, who gave their unflinching support to the fulfillment of this long-awaited exhibition.

Most fundamentally, we are all grateful to Georgia O'Keeffe for making such significant art.

David Turner
Associate Director
Museum of Fine Arts
Santa Fe, New Mexico

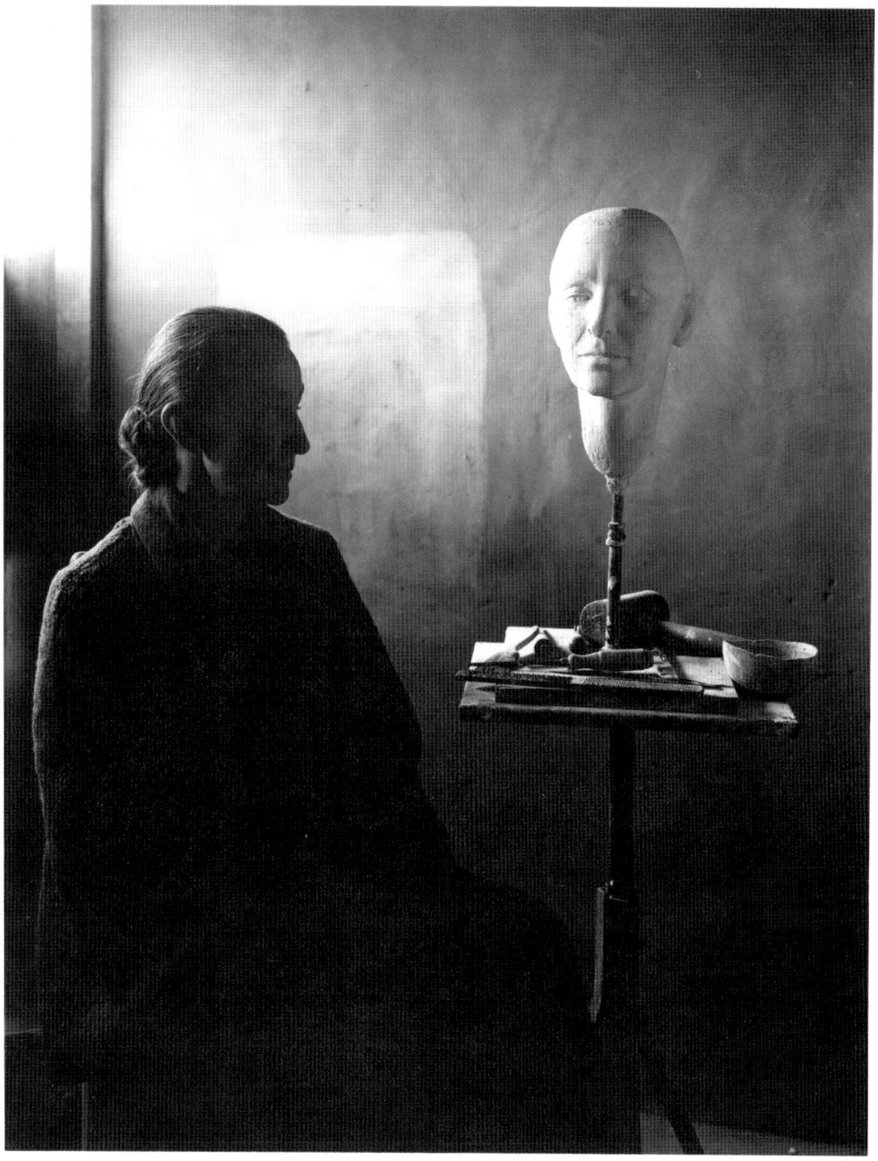

Georgia O'Keeffe, Abiquiu, New Mexico (Bust of O'Keeffe by Mary Callery), 1945. Photograph by Eliot Porter. Future Gift to the Museum of Fine Arts, Museum of New Mexico from the collection of Gil Hitchcock.

GEORGIA O'KEEFFE
WORKS ON PAPER
A CRITICAL ESSAY

Virtually from the beginning of Georgia O'Keeffe's career, her aura has extended beyond the confines of the art world. In recent decades she has attained the status of cultural heroine akin to that of a movie star. The myth surrounding her, precipitated and encouraged by Alfred Stieglitz' photographs of her, has been sustained by her extraordinary physical presence and by the manner in which she has chosen to live her life. Yet while these factors fuel the public's long-standing fascination for her art, they do not explain it. And, finally, they are peripheral, for the secret of O'Keeffe's allure lies ultimately in the power and originality of her style and in the extraordinary capacity of her images to communicate something of significance to her audience.

The following discussion deals with O'Keeffe's works on paper. Although she is known primarily as a painter, her earliest mature works were exclusively on paper; they provide valuable insights into the origins of her vocabulary and basic approach to art. Indeed, it was these works which led to her first exhibitions in New York and on which her initial acclaim was based. Although O'Keeffe's intense commitment to drawing and watercolor decreased after she turned to oil in 1918, it resumed in the 1960s and 1970s when the formal simplicity and expansiveness of her work reached perhaps its fullest expression.

O'Keeffe was born in Sun Prairie, Wisconsin, in 1887. After graduating from high school in Virginia, where her family had moved in 1901, she attended the School of The Art Institute of Chicago for a year. This was followed by a year in New York City at the Art Students League, then dominated by William Merritt Chase. Within this period she apparently experimented with a number of different styles and media (plates 1, 2, 3). After these experiences she worked as a commercial artist in Chicago for two years, during which time she stopped painting, feeling it was better to abandon art altogether than merely to imitate what others had already done.

Following her return to her family in Virginia in the summer of 1912, her sister persuaded her to take an art course taught by Alon Bement at the University of Virginia's Summer School. This course changed her life. Although O'Keeffe had been exposed to a smattering of modern art while studying at the League and had seen at least two contemporary art exhibitions—those of Auguste Rodin and Henri Matisse at Stieglitz' gallery 291—it was Bement who introduced her to an aesthetic system that liberated her creativity. A disciple of the distinguished educator Arthur Wesley Dow, whose theories drew upon Gauguin and Oriental art, Bement served as a conduit for Dow's belief in the principles of abstract design and the pictorial expression of emotions.[1] It was Bement who directed O'Keeffe to Kandinsky's landmark book *Concerning the Spiritual in Art* and to Arthur Jerome Eddy's *Cubism and Post-Impressionism*, which contained her first view of Arthur Dove's abstractions of natural forms. O'Keeffe's acceptance and assimilation of these ideas were strengthened over the next four years with her return to the University of Virginia to teach summer school with Bement.

Important though Bement was for the development of O'Keeffe's art, even more critical was her decision to go to New York for the 1914–15 school term and enroll in Dow's class at Teachers College, Columbia University. Here she became steeped in Dow's teaching, which advocated replacing Western painting's three-dimensional illusionism with a system based on tonally balanced contrasts of light and dark and flattened, stylized designs such as those found in Chinese and Japanese art. Unlike her earlier experience in New York, during this stay O'Keeffe took full advantage of the city's aesthetic offerings, frequenting Stieglitz' gallery with fellow student Anita Pollitzer and absorbing the array of European and American modern art exhibited there.

By the time O'Keeffe left New York and assumed her teaching post in the fall of 1915 in Columbia, South Carolina, she was well enough versed in contemporary art to have purchased a copy of Kandinsky's *Concerning the Spiritual in Art* and to be subscribing to *The Masses* and Stieglitz' magazine, *Camera Work*. These facts belie the prevalent assumption that O'Keeffe executed her first mature works in total ignorance of advanced European and American art. Yet, as O'Keeffe astutely observed later about these early influences, "you pick up ideas here and there. If you mention any particular source, it gives that too much emphasis."[2] Indeed, none of her contacts with the modernist theories being expounded in the early years of the century can account for the extraordinary group of charcoal drawings she executed that fall—drawings whose authenticity and singularity justifiably catapulted her into the highest ranks of American artists.

In the drawings O'Keeffe produced in the fall of 1915, she renounced the color explosions of the previous months and limited herself to black and white. Despite their restricted palette, these works show O'Keeffe's remarkable control over the balancing of light and dark tonalities. She played subtle gradations of gray, black, and white against darker strokes of charcoal to create complex and richly modulated compositions. Although their imagery is uniquely O'Keeffe's, these charcoals shared with the American Arts and Crafts Movement a vocabulary of stylized, curvilinear motifs which alluded to nature. Perhaps it was her study with Bement and Dow that provided an alternative to Cubism. But whatever the cause, O'Keeffe, unlike most of her

1. Dow had studied with Gauguin and The Nabis at Pont-Avon and was a colleague of the brilliant orientalist Ernest Fenollosa.

2. Quoted in Calvin Tomkins, "Profiles: The Rose in the Eye Looked Pretty Fine," *The New Yorker* (March 4, 1974): 47.

contemporaries, managed to bypass the ubiquitous rectilinearity of the French style and achieve a full-blown abstraction which was emotive and non-geometric. Her use of organically allusive shapes was neither gratuitous nor superficial, but emerged out of a deeply felt connection to nature. Simplified in most cases to a centralized, dominant motif around which other forms swirl, her images pulse with the rhythms and dynamism of nature itself.

O'Keeffe shipped these charcoals to Anita Pollitzer in December. Disregarding O'Keeffe's admonition not to show them to anyone, Pollitzer took them to Stieglitz, whose gallery she and O'Keeffe had visited regularly the previous year. Stieglitz responded positively to the drawings and wrote to O'Keeffe. Buoyed perhaps by Stieglitz' appreciation of her work, or perhaps simply by a desire for greater aesthetic stimulation than that offered in South Carolina, O'Keeffe left her teaching post in February 1916 and returned to New York to enroll again in Dow's class on teaching methods. Although she viewed exhibitions at Stieglitz' gallery throughout the semester, O'Keeffe seems to have had little personal contact with him over the next six months, for he included her drawings in a May group exhibition at 291 without her knowledge. Angry at not being consulted and nervous about having work on view which seemed to her so personal, O'Keeffe made her now legendary pilgrimage to the gallery to demand that Stieglitz remove her work. His convincing arguments for keeping the drawings on view cemented the beginning of one of the most productive personal relationships in the annals of American art.

By the time O'Keeffe returned to the University of Virginia in June for what proved to be her last teaching session with Bement, she felt confident enough about her mastery of drawing to reintroduce color into her compositions. One of her first experiments was *Blue Lines*. Drawn initially in charcoal, the motif was refined in a series of five or six works using black watercolor (figure 1) before appearing in its final version in blue watercolor. Rising vertically from a broad horizontal base, the image possesses that extraordinary duality which permeates the best of O'Keeffe's work: it is at once lyrical and restrained; bold and subtle. As with her other watercolors from this period, it is an abstraction richly imbued with landscape allusions. F. S. C. Northrop, as if in recognition of O'Keeffe's familiarity with Oriental art through Dow's teaching, later used the watercolor as the frontispiece to his book, *The Meeting of East and West*. In the book he quoted Stieglitz' interpretation of *Blue Lines* as being a representation of the male and female sensibilities, emerging from a common base and following distinct, yet mutually interdependent courses.

O'Keeffe continued to work almost exclusively in watercolor after her arrival in Canyon, Texas, in 1916 to teach at the West Texas Normal School. While she experimented occasionally with recognizable images—for example, *Roof with Snow* and *Seated Nude* X1 (figure 2, plate 15)—the overwhelming majority of her watercolor subjects were abstractions of natural motifs (figure 3, plates 12, 13). Following Dow's technique of exploring several solutions to the same problem, O'Keeffe worked on most of these images in multiple versions (figure 4, plates 5, 6). In contrast to the juxtaposition of curvilinear and rectilinear shapes in her charcoals, these watercolors relied almost exclusively on a vocabulary of organic forms. As in her series *Blue* I–*Blue* IV, she

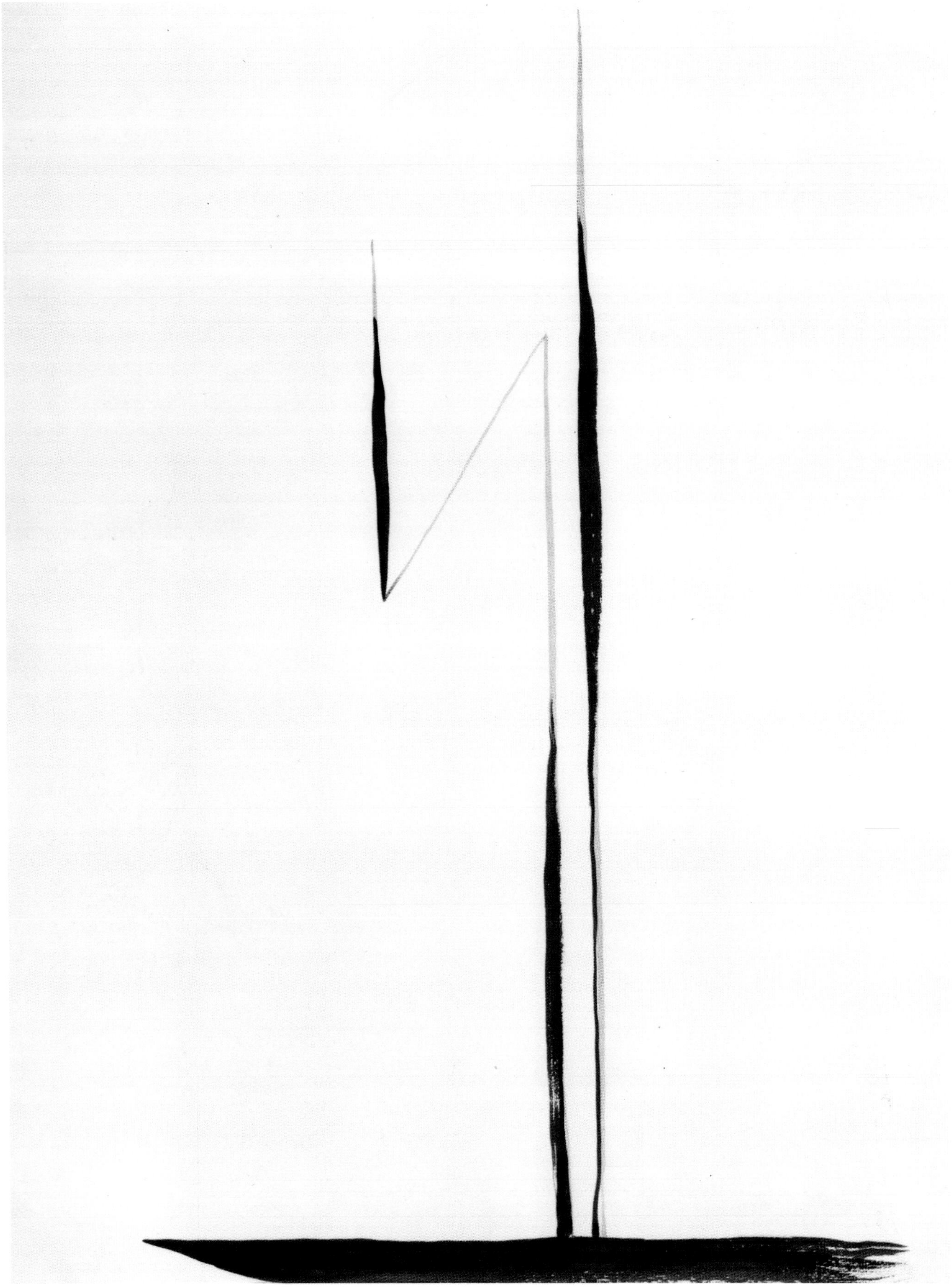

Figure 1. *Black Lines*, 1916, watercolor, 25 x 19 inches, Courtesy of Andrew Crispo Gallery

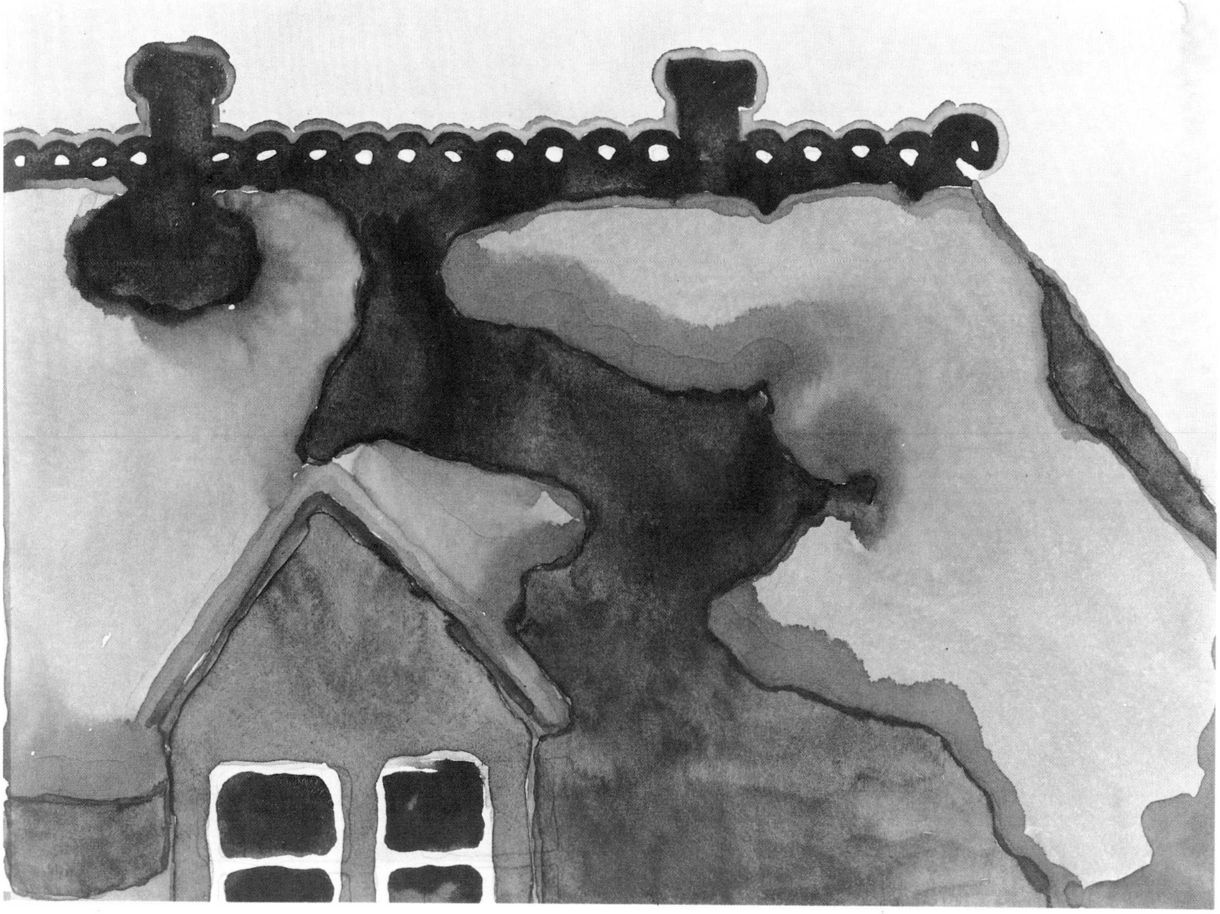

Figure 2. *Roof with Snow,* 1917, watercolor, 9 x 12 inches, Amarillo Art Center

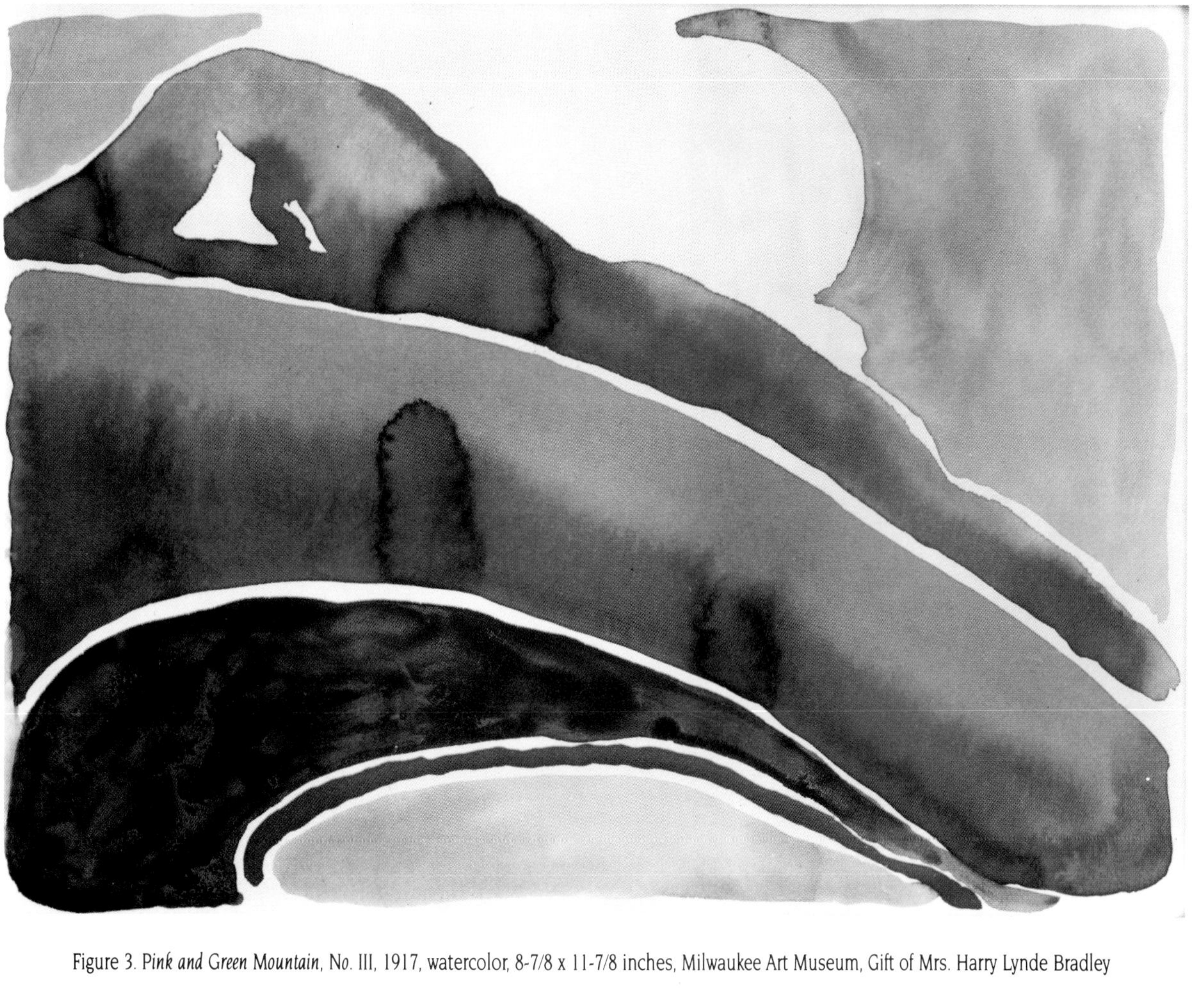

Figure 3. *Pink and Green Mountain,* No. III, 1917, watercolor, 8-7/8 x 11-7/8 inches, Milwaukee Art Museum, Gift of Mrs. Harry Lynde Bradley

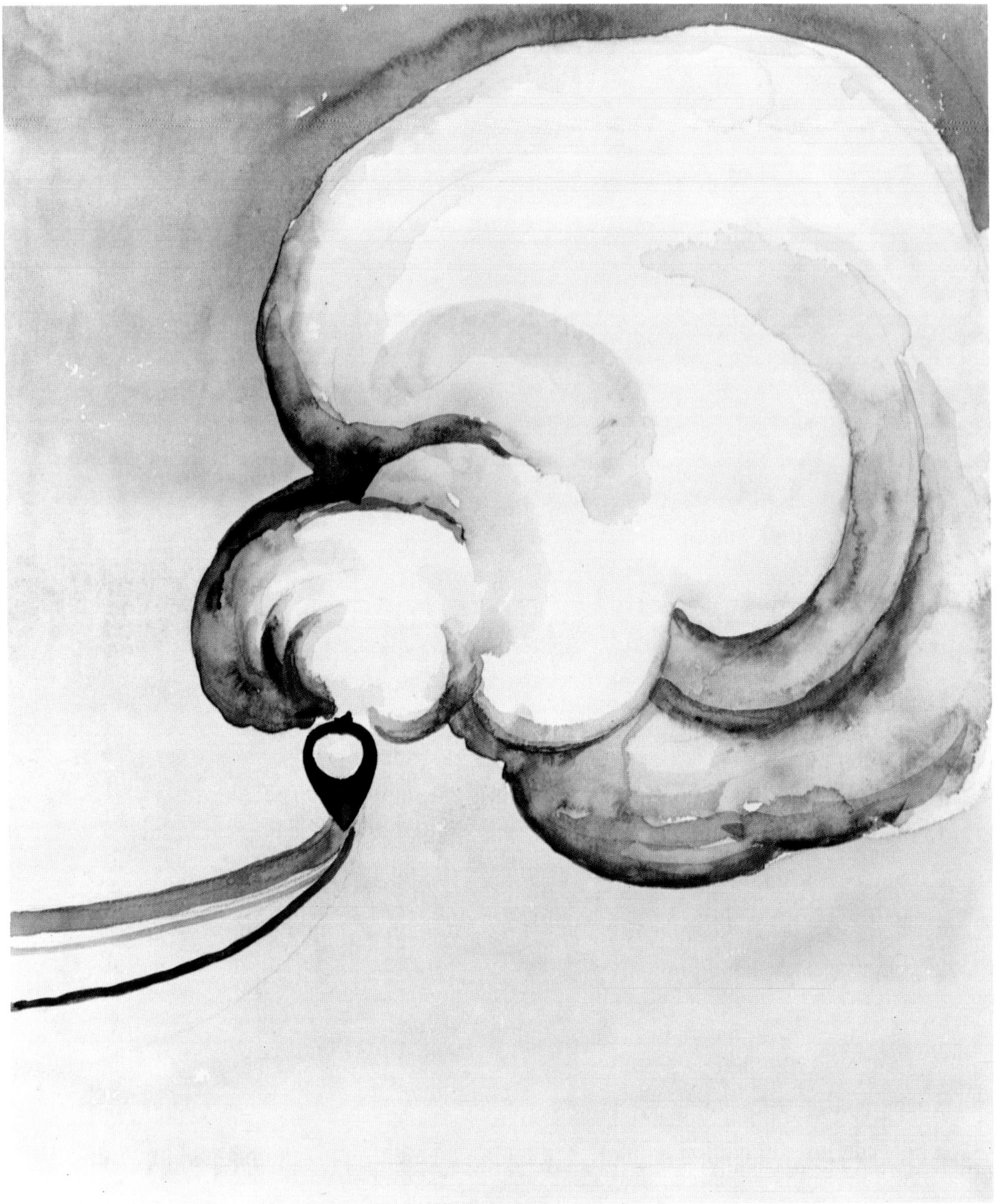

Figure 4. *Train Coming In—Canyon, Texas*, ca. 1918, watercolor, 12 x 9 inches, Amarillo Art Center

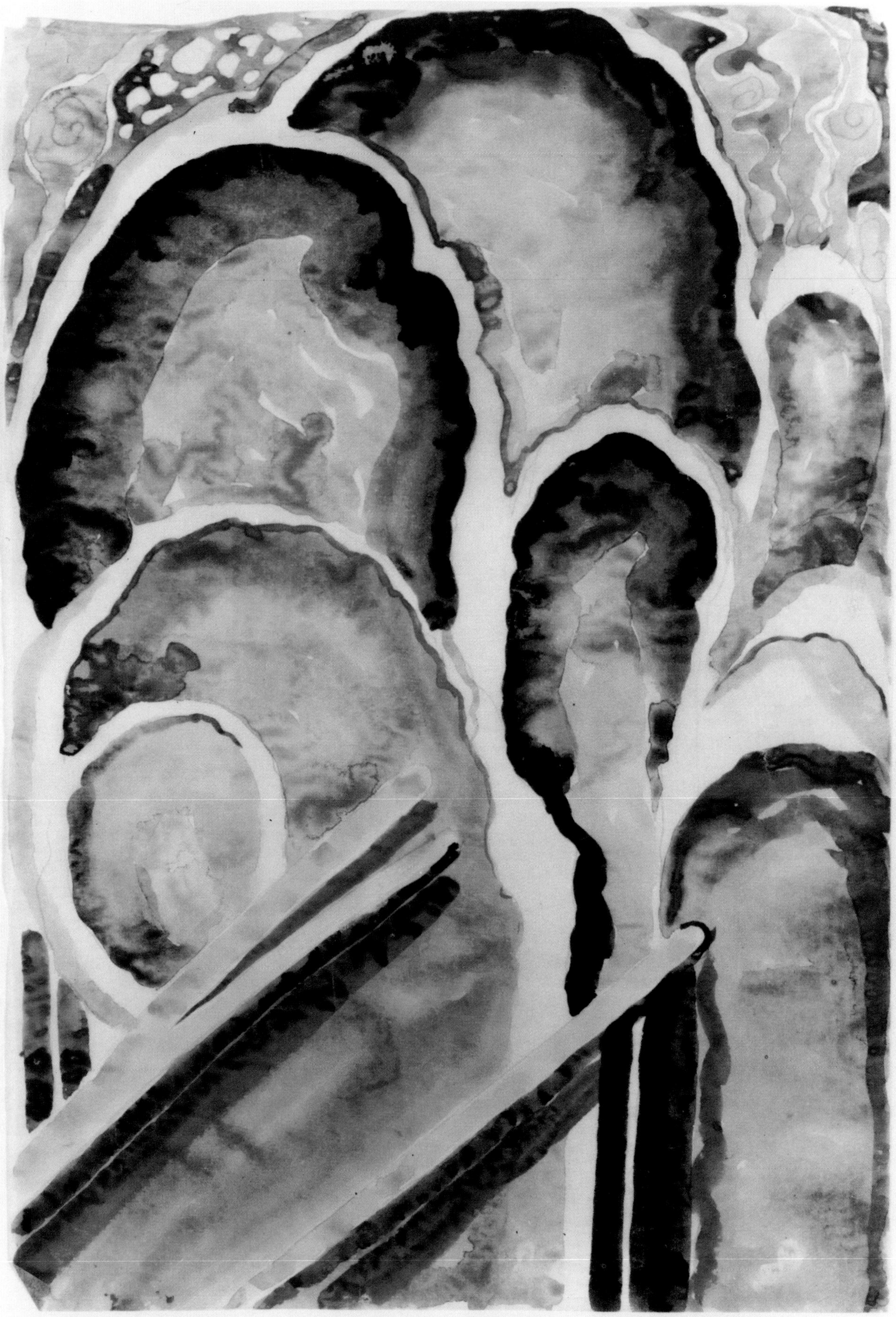

Figure 5. *Blue #1*, 1916, watercolor, 16 x 11 inches, The Brooklyn Museum, Bequest of Mary T. Cockcroft

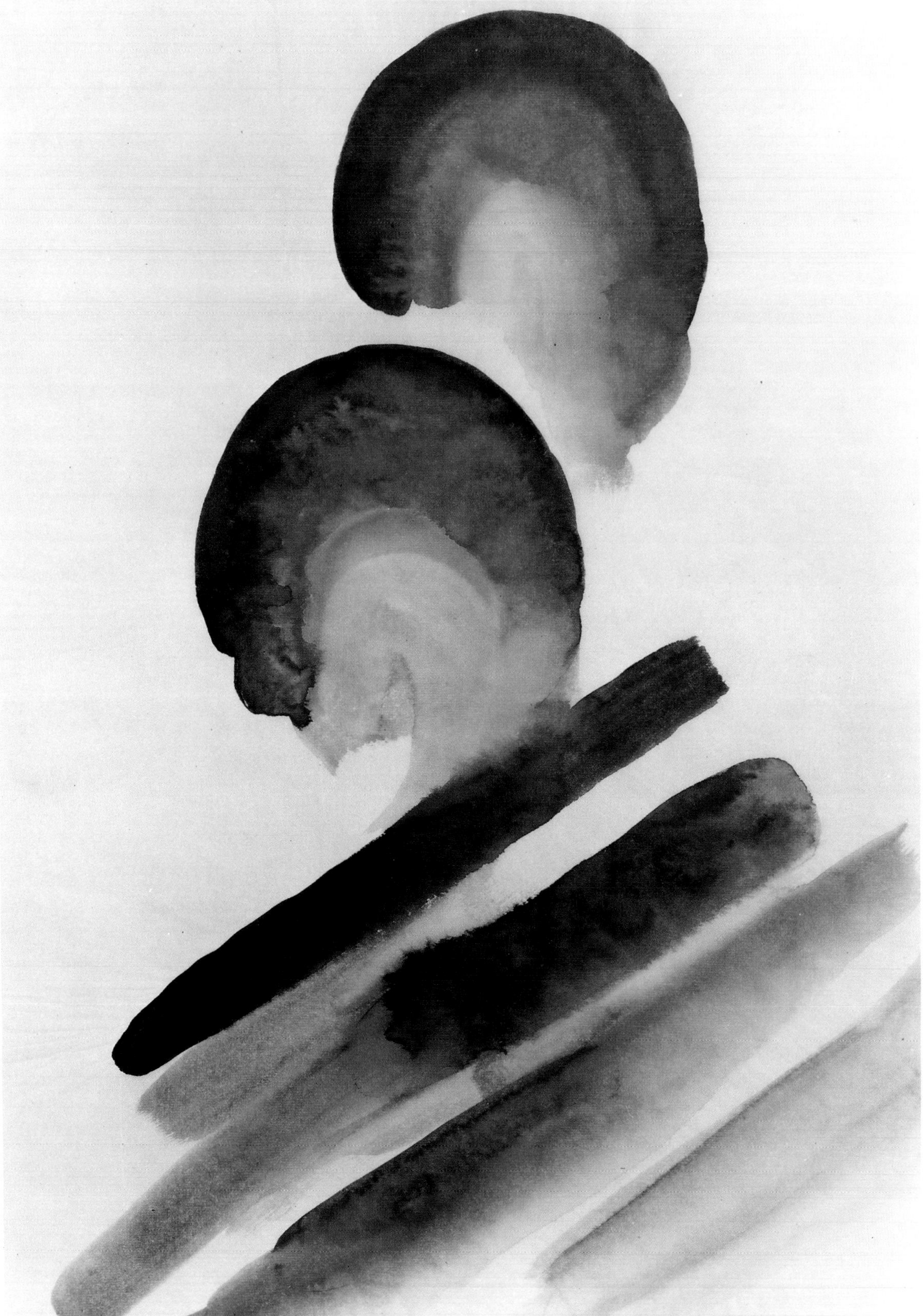

Figure 6. *Blue #2*, 1916, watercolor, 15-7/8 x 10-15/16 inches, The Brooklyn Museum, Bequest of Mary T. Cockcroft

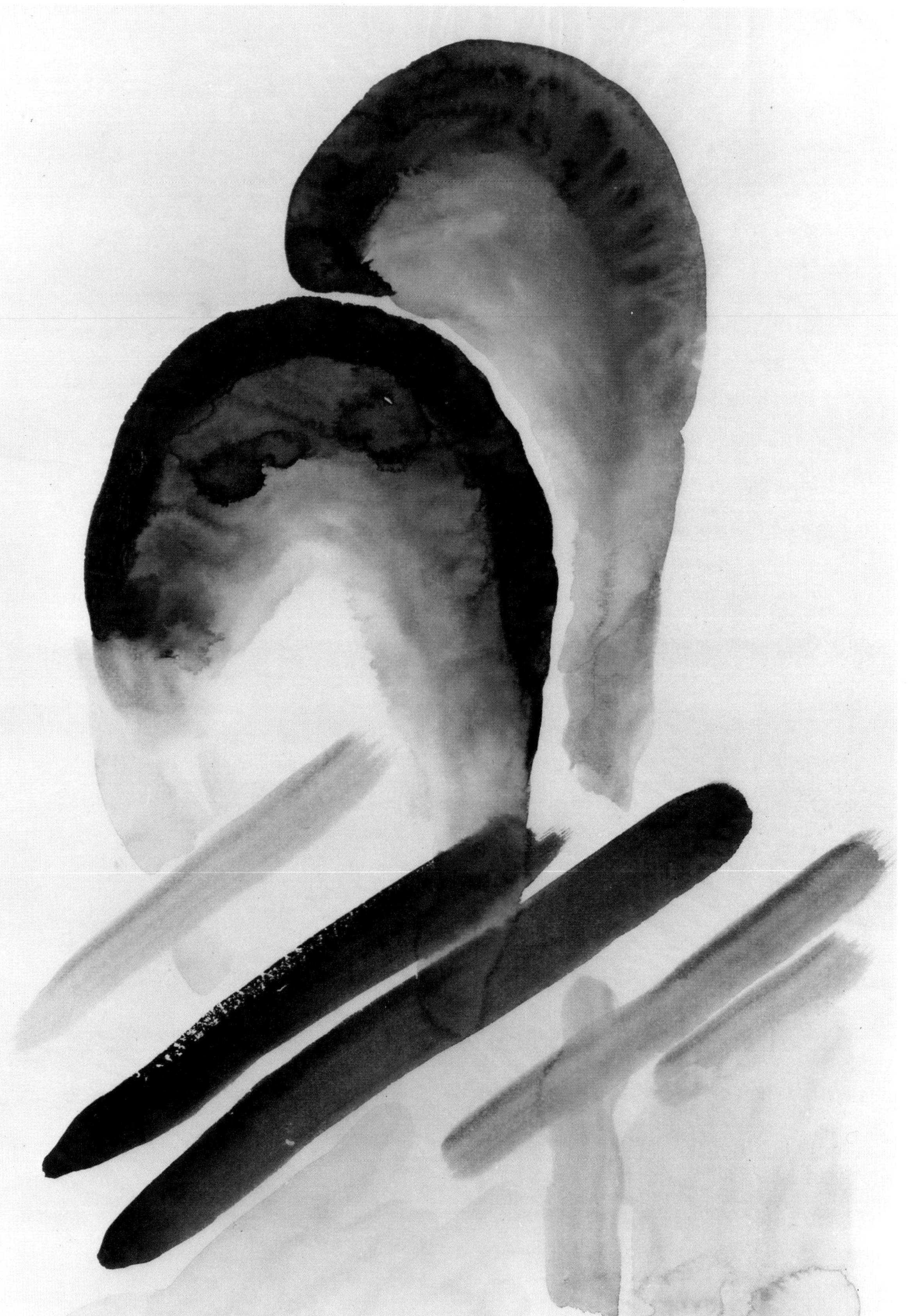

Figure 7. *Blue #3*, 1916, watercolor, 15-15/16 x 10-15/16 inches, The Brooklyn Museum, Bequest of Mary T. Cockcroft

relinquished the flat patterning and stylization of the charcoals in favor of a rhapsodic celebration of the vital, generative forces of nature (figures 5, 6, 7, plate 7). One senses in these watercolors the joy that O'Keeffe felt for the expansive space and grandeur of the west Texas landscape.

O'Keeffe's view of the American landscape was an undeniably romantic one; yet it is to the unfettered freedom of the sky rather than the circumscribed boundaries of the earth that these works address themselves. Such feelings for the timelessness and infinite expanse of the sky were to remain with O'Keeffe throughout her career. She remarked in later years that she was "not a pavement person," and in her 1944 exhibition catalogue she identified the blue sky seen through the holes in her pelvic bone paintings as "that Blue that will always be there as it is now after all man's destruction is finished."[3] As if a corollary to her sense of this infinity, O'Keeffe extended her watercolor motifs so that they filled the entire paper, treating them as neither autonomous nor finite, but part of a larger, embracing totality (plate 9).

O'Keeffe's watercolors not only established her basic approach to the simplification of nature but her talents as a colorist as well. Throughout her career, she seemed able to invent new colors or to combine known colors in fresh ways. To her, color was an essential rather than a peripheral entity. It dominated her perception and descriptions of objects and events. Even her black and white works, as Paul Strand noted in his 1924 article on her work, seemed to have been felt by her as color.[4] In her oil paintings her colors are finely chiseled and palpable; in her watercolors she deftly exploited the medium so that colors bleed into one another, producing mottled surfaces and subtle variations of tone within color areas. Her juxtaposition of warm and cool colors and their treatment as projecting and receding shapes impart the sense of a moving, breathing surface. Her first watercolors, from the summer of 1916, rely on the tonal modulations of single colors, as in *Blue* I–*Blue* IV (figures 5, 6, 7, plate 7). Later in the summer, she began combining two or three highly saturated complementary colors—red, blue, and green. In works such as *Red, Blue, and Green*, she controlled the amount of water added to the medium in order to create tonally diffuse atmospheres (plate 10); in other works, such as the *Evening Star* series, she separated the colored zones with thin bands of unpainted paper, thereby preventing the colors' optical mix and heightening their brilliance and luminosity (plates 18–22).

Although O'Keeffe's visits to Stieglitz' gallery during the winter and spring of 1916 had strengthened her knowledge of European and American modern art, she nevertheless had created her watercolors independently, without affiliating herself to any school or theory. It was as if, having decided to forgo the conventions of art and make work simply to satisfy herself, her images arose out of some kind of inner

3. Georgia O'Keeffe, conversation with the author, March 1981; Georgia O'Keeffe, "About Painting Desert Bones," *Georgia O'Keeffe: Paintings—1943* (New York: An American Place, 1944), unpaginated.

4. Paul Strand, "Georgia O'Keeffe," *Playboy: A Portfolio of Art and Satire*, 9 (July 1924): 16, 19, 20.

vision and necessity. They were, as she later wrote, "often the most definite form for the intangible thing in myself that I can only clarify in paint."[5] What appeared to others to be abstract was, to her, starkly revealing, a conviction which accounted for her early reticence about exhibiting her work. "I have painted portraits that to me are almost photographic. I remember hesitating to show the paintings, they looked so real to me. But they have passed into the world as abstractions—no one seeing what they are."[6]

O'Keeffe's desire to reproduce the essence of an object rather than its external form and to express the inner self held high favor within Stieglitz' circle of artists. O'Keeffe could well have absorbed these ideas, even if only obliquely, from *Camera Work* and Eddy's *Cubism and Post-Impressionism*. Yet what she created went far beyond what had been done previously. As abstract equivalents of inner emotional states, her watercolors attained the "condition of music" which Kandinsky championed as the essence of abstraction in *Concerning the Spiritual in Art*. That they did so using a vocabulary grounded in a spiritual appreciation of the landscape identifies them as distinctly American.

While O'Keeffe was making her watercolors and teaching in Texas during the 1916–17 school year, she had corresponded with Stieglitz and sent him works which formed the basis of her first solo show at 291. The exhibition, which opened on April 3, 1917, three days before the United States declared war on Germany, signaled the beginning of Stieglitz' lifelong association with O'Keeffe, but it also marked the end of an important era in American art—the permanent closing of 291.

A year after O'Keeffe's exhibition, Stieglitz persuaded her to leave Texas and come to New York. It was an important decision: not only did it bring her close to perhaps the best artists and minds of the time, but her contact with Stieglitz, whom she married in 1924, generated greater confidence in herself as an artist. She began working primarily in oil, enlarging the scale of her work and heightening its palette. When she did use paper her medium was pastel and charcoal, a preference she maintained throughout the 1950s. By using pastel and charcoal, she forfeited the fluidity and transparency of watercolor in favor of a velvety surface and more controlled handling. In imagery, she replaced the expansive forms of her watercolors with tighter, more focused compositions which exhibit the same daring juxtaposition of color and the same precise delineation of forms and contours as her concurrent oils. Her pastel subjects during the 1920s ranged from abstractions such as *Lake George and Woods* (plate 25) to more well-known floral studies and city scenes such as *New York Rooftops* and *East River with Sun* (plates 27, 28). In her first portrayals of flowers—for example *Canna Lily* and *Red Canna* (plates 23, 24)—she treated the flowers as isolated and finite. Even after she enlarged and cropped the image so that it filled the entire paper sheet, as in *Narcissa's Last Orchid*, her compositions remained centralized and her forms tightly compacted (plate 32).

5. Georgia O'Keeffe, *Georgia O'Keeffe* (New York: The Viking Press, 1976), unpaginated.

6. Ibid.

Critical reaction to O'Keeffe's works throughout the twenties was immensely favorable. Early commentators extolled the emotional underpinnings of her work and its evocative pictorial language. Her work was viewed as the embodiment of intelligence and intuition, and as quintessentially American. More disquieting to her were the attributions of erotic or sexual symbolism. Since many of these interpretations originated among denizens of Stieglitz' circle, it is likely that Stieglitz himself was a major culprit in expounding this view. Regardless of how legitimate such interpretations seemed in the context of the period, they did obscure the strength and originality of O'Keeffe's formal innovations. The balance was not redressed until the 1960s, when critics began to discuss her work in terms of composition and color.

The three decades after 1930 saw a marked reduction in O'Keeffe's output of works on paper. With the exception of a few landscapes, flowers, and depictions of starkly isolated objects (figures 8, 9, 10, plates 29, 30, 31), she concentrated her energies on oil painting. In these works she continued her magnified flower motifs while simultaneously developing a powerful, iconic subject matter based on the imagery of New Mexico, where she began summering in 1929. Not only did the limitless boundaries and visual severity of this landscape offer a ready pictorial analogue for her sense of infinity and timelessness, but the Spanish-American crosses and the sun-bleached skulls and pelvic bones she observed there became the sources for an iconography of continuity and hope. Yet only occasionally did these images find expression in her pastels.

Following the death of Alfred Stieglitz in 1946, O'Keeffe established permanent residency in New Mexico. Her paintings henceforth assumed an extreme simplification of form and an almost decorative flatness, as exemplified in her *Patio Door* series, which she executed throughout the 1950s. She advanced further toward formal economy in 1959 with a group of ten depictions of riverbeds drawn in charcoal, her first sustained use of the medium since 1916 (plate 36). These drawings emerged out of O'Keeffe's habit of deriving landscape images from a high vantage point. This proclivity made her notice the riverbeds visible from a hill near her house at Ghost Ranch. When her schedule after Stieglitz' death began to include more air travel, memories of those riverbeds primed her for an appreciation of aerial views of meandering rivers and tributaries—views which became the basis for a new series of radically simplified compositions. Drawn first as 1-1/2-inch-square pencil sketches, then elaborated into charcoals and later into oils, they exhibit the same frontality and attenuated vertical accent that marked her earlier watercolors, *Blue Lines* and *Black Lines* (figure 1). In their flatness and curvilinear patterning, these charcoals also recall her 1915–16 charcoal series. Although the same equivocation between abstraction and nature permeates both groups, the sense of frontality is so strong in the river drawings that they are as readily perceived as depictions of trees as of rivers. Indeed, it was this flattened space and insistently frontal presentation, coupled with O'Keeffe's starkly reductivist vocabulary, that made this and subsequent work seem so contemporary in the context of Minimal art, which emerged in the mid-1960s. One reason for the greater two-dimensionality of space in the river series was that O'Keeffe's handling of the charcoal medium was now softer and more homogeneous, less prone to dramatic contrasts of light against dark and line against plane. Rather than filling the entire page, as she had often done with her earlier charcoals, she balanced the river motif against the empty, white ground of the paper. Despite the starkness of her imagery,

O'Keeffe managed to evoke the sense of expansive space which had characterized her first charcoal series by means of a linear network that connected opposing edges of the paper. In this way she restated the themes of infinity and continuity with which she had begun her career.

In her work after 1960, O'Keeffe returned not only to the themes but to the shapes and rhythms she had first expressed in her drawings and watercolors from 1915 to 1918. The relation between her river charcoals and *Blue Lines* was but one in a series of flashbacks during these years. Just as the sky predominated in her earlier watercolors, so were clouds the primary subject matter in her paintings in the sixties. Moreover, these cloud paintings used the same mosaic organization of flattened oval shapes that had appeared in charcoal drawings from 1916, while her 1922 pastel *Lightning At Sea* (figure 11) morphologically predates her later involvement with aerial landscapes. Finally, her awesome rock paintings of the 1970s hark back to drawings such as *Untitled 3* (formerly *My Heart*) (1944) (plate 33). Although the absence of magnification and a scale-defining horizon line deprived these earlier depictions of the solidity and monumental presence of their oil-on-canvas counterparts, they nevertheless exhibit the same isolation, purity of form, and emphatic contour as their subsequent progeny. This capacity to find nourishment in a few central impulses throughout a lifetime was shared by other artists in the Stieglitz circle. Arthur Dove's notion that, "One so seldom gets a good breeder idea. Two or three in a lifetime would be enormous," was echoed in O'Keeffe's statement that "each person has only a few shapes in their head."[7] That O'Keeffe created such a powerful legacy from these shapes attests to her authenticity and originality as an artist.

As O'Keeffe's eyesight began to fail in the 1970s, her work became increasingly simplified. She turned again to the watercolor medium, employing it in combinations of highly saturated colors as she had done earlier. By using discreet single images isolated on the paper, she replaced the atmospheric effusions of her earlier experiments with a refined calligraphic grace and serenity (plate 37). Executed with single, broad strokes, these works share with Zen drawings a concentrated intensity and control that draw upon inner resources rather than external stimulation. As with her last series of paintings, *A Day with Juan*, these works are divorced from finite subject matter and the material concerns of the world. In their authority and self-containment they stand as correlatives to O'Keeffe's vision of "how wonderful it would be to simply stand out in space and have nothing."[8]

Barbara Haskell
Curator
Whitney Museum of American Art
New York City

7. Quoted in Frederick S. Wight, *Arthur G. Dove* (Los Angeles: University of California Art Galleries, 1958), p. 64; O'Keeffe, conversation with the author, March 1981.

8. Quoted in Charles C. Eldredge III, "Georgia O'Keeffe: The Development of an American Modern," Ph.D. dissertation, University of Minnesota, 1971, p. 127.

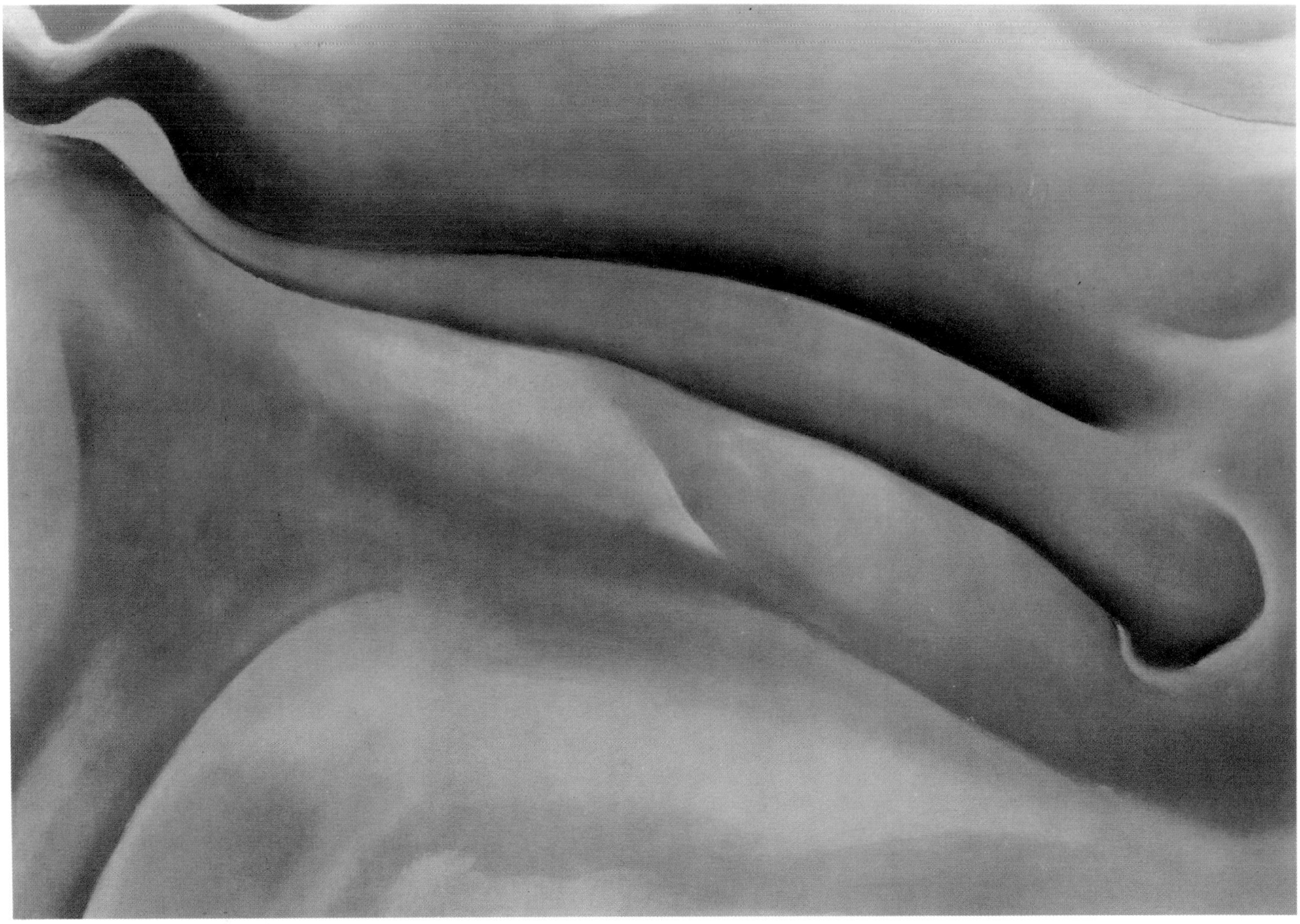

Figure 8. *Shell No. 1*, 1932, pastel, 9-3/4 x 14-3/4 inches, Courtesy of Hirschl and Adler Galleries, Inc., New York

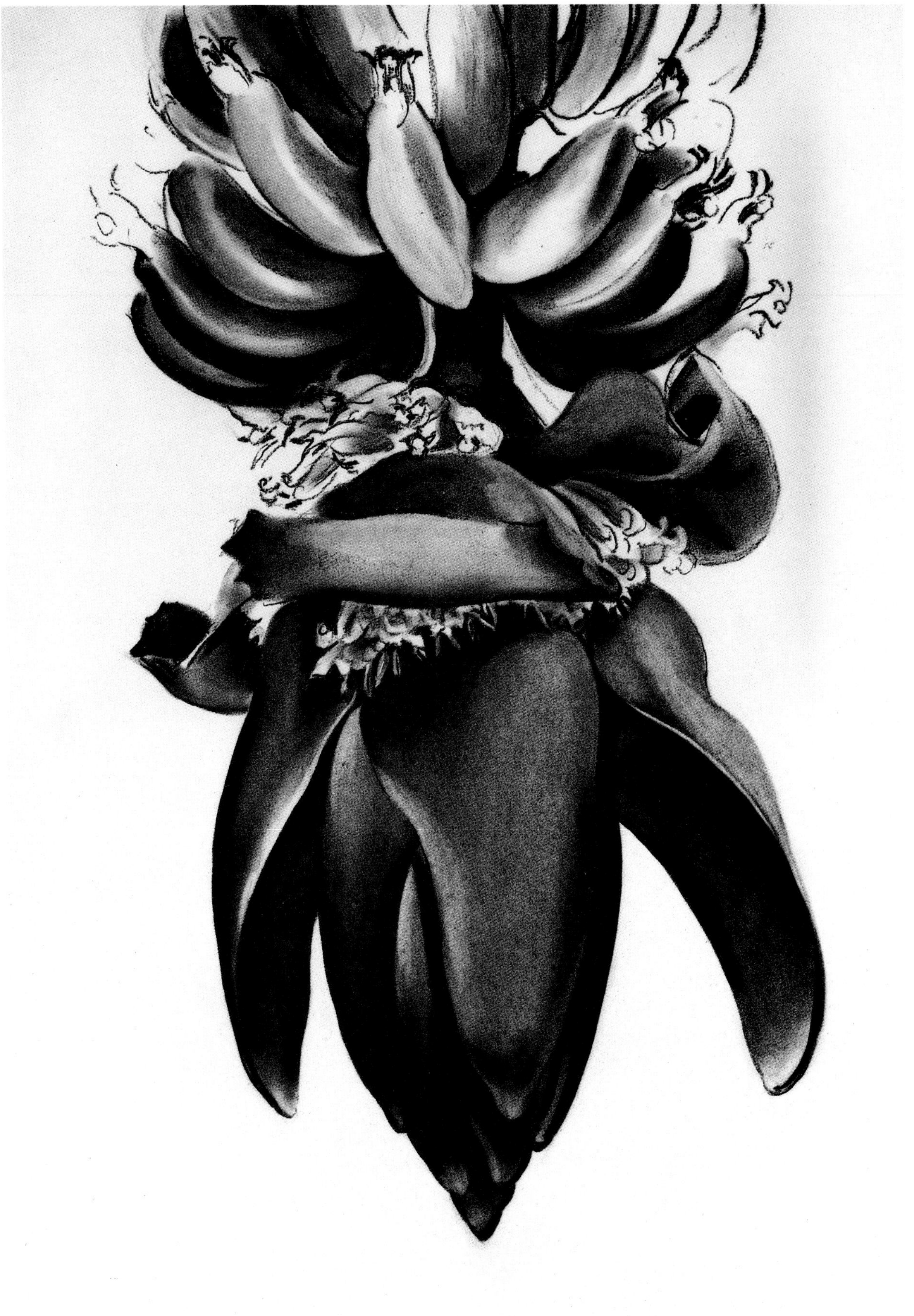

Figure 9. *Banana Flower* No. 1, 1933, charcoal, 22 x 15 inches, The Arkansas Arts Center Foundation Collection

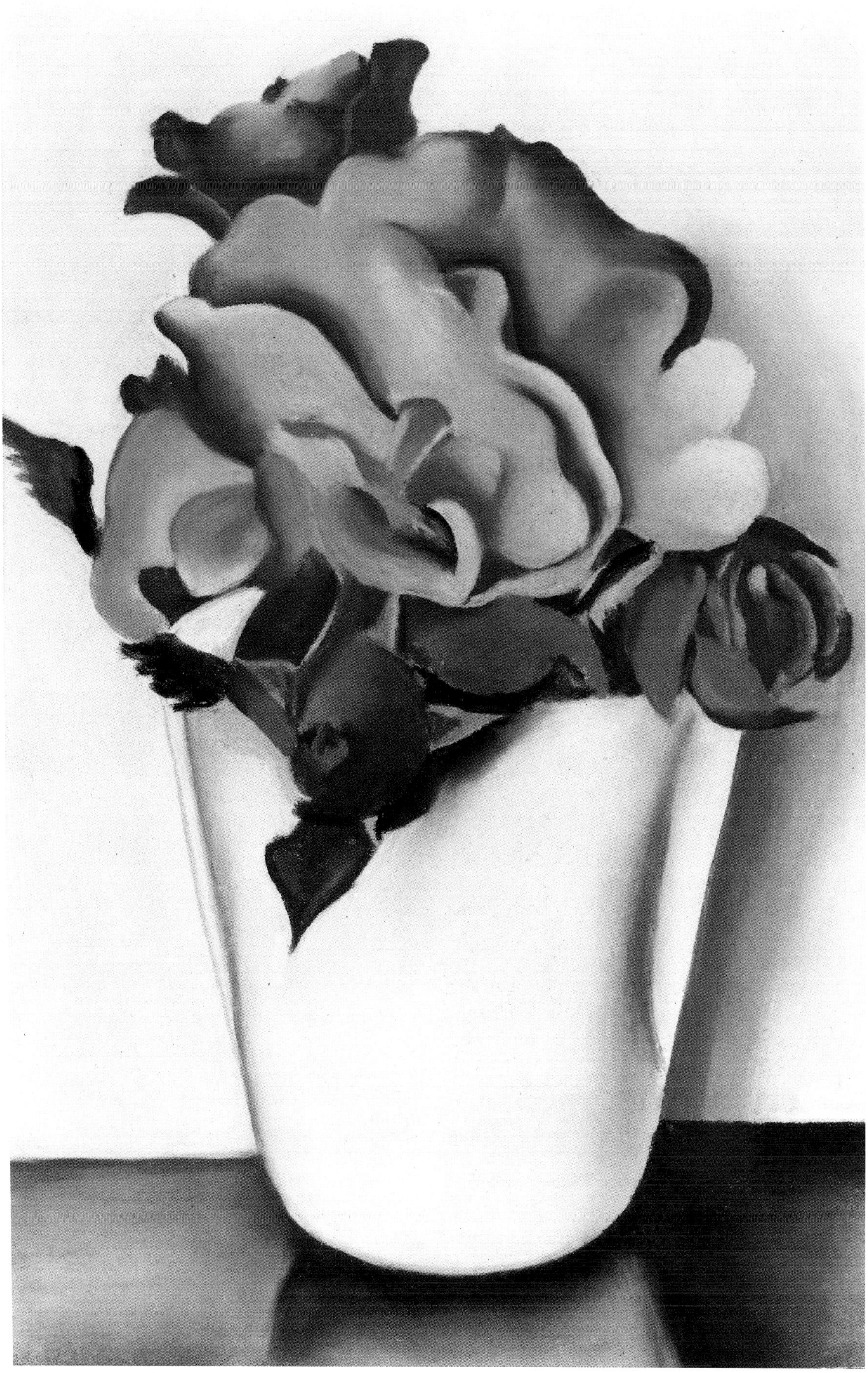

Figure 10. *Roses*, 1934, pastel, 17-1/2 x 12 inches, Beinecke Rare Book and Manuscript Library, Yale University

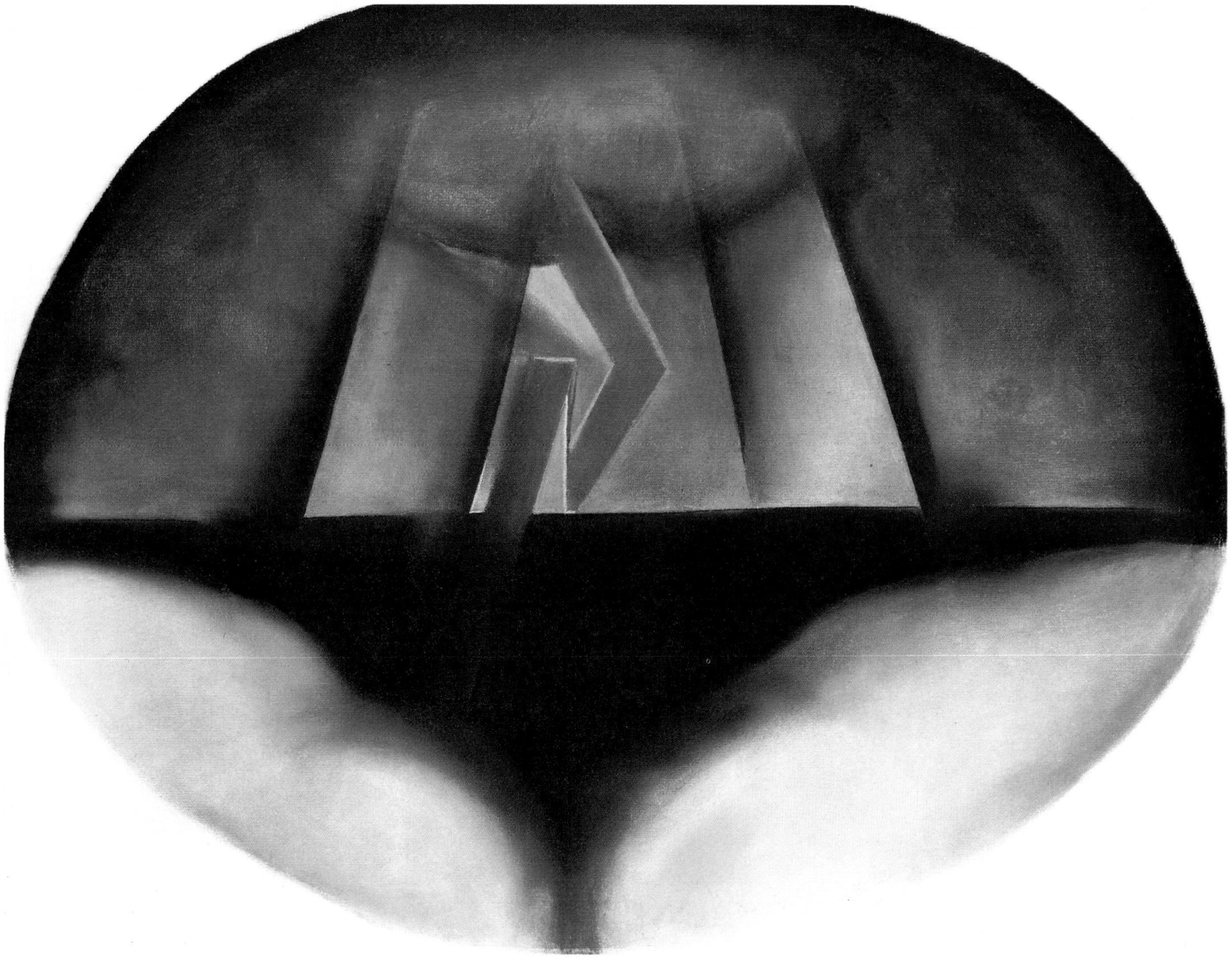

Figure 11. *Lightning at Sea*, 1922, pastel, 19 x 25-1/2 inches, The Lane Collection

GEORGIA O'KEEFFE

WORKS ON PAPER

Plate 1. *Lady with Red Hair*, ca. 1910, linoleum block print, 7-1/2 x 7 inches, Courtesy of Gerald Peters Gallery, Santa Fe

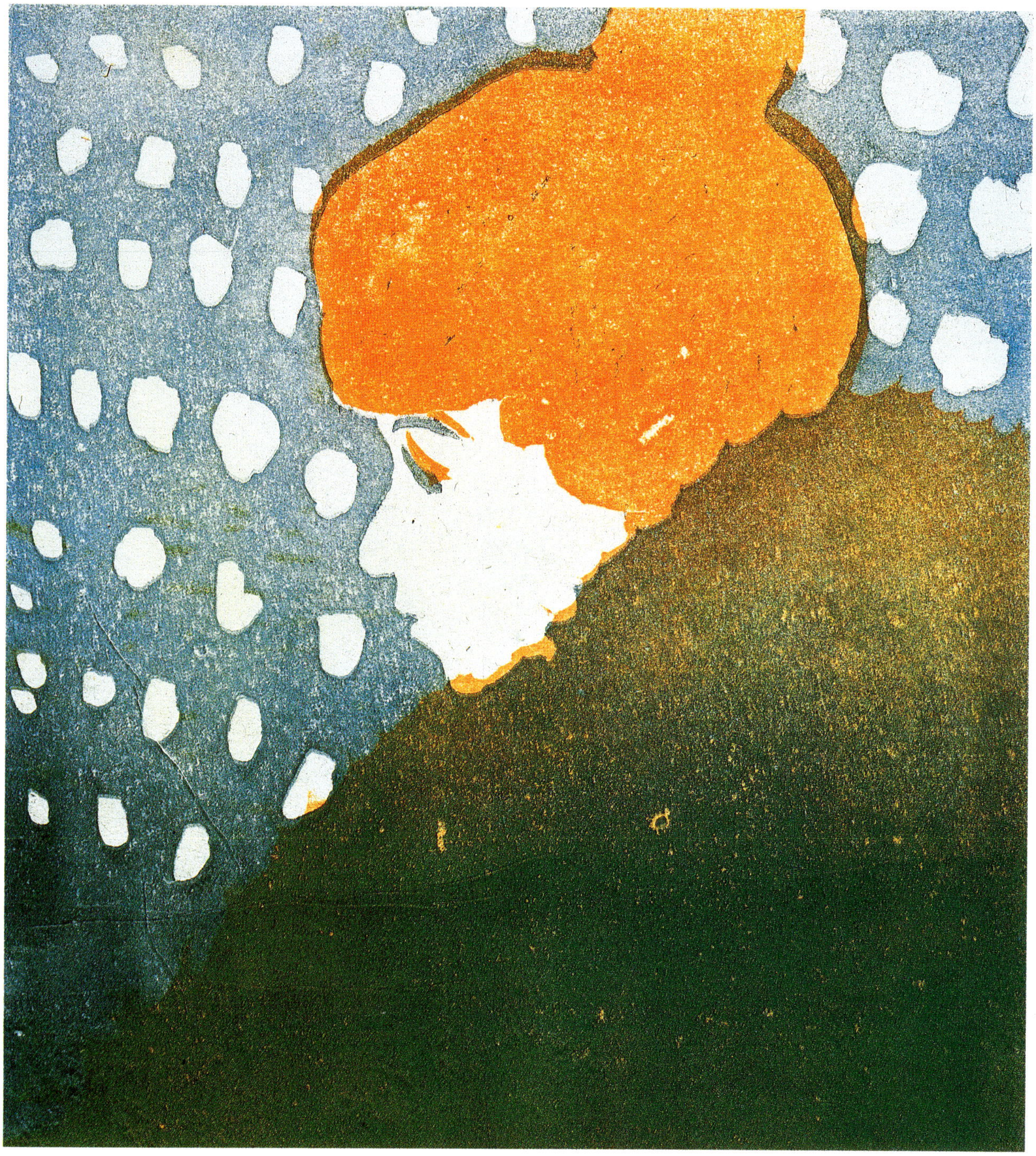

Plate 2. ***Untitled Portrait***, before 1917, monotype, 4 x 3 inches, Anonymous loan

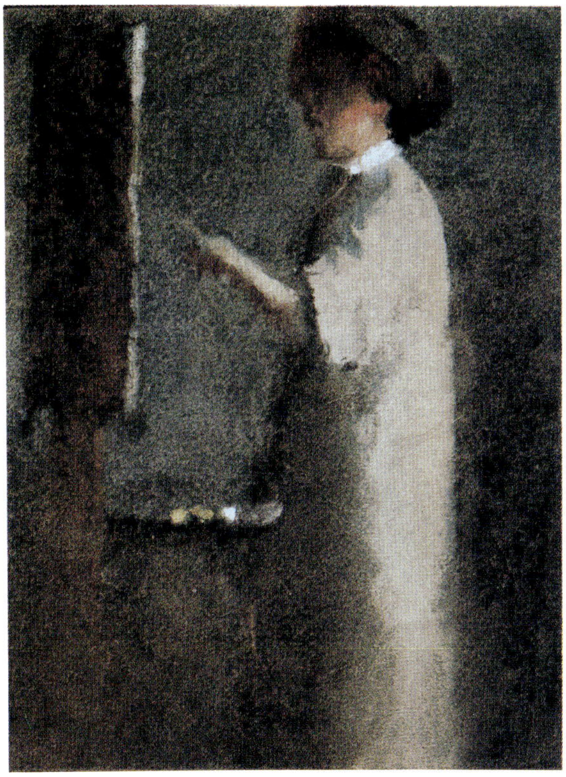

Plate 3. *Still Life*, before 1915, watercolor, 20-1/4 x 14-1/8 inches, Elvehjem Museum of Art, University of Wisconsin—Madison, Gift of Hermine Sauthoff Davidson

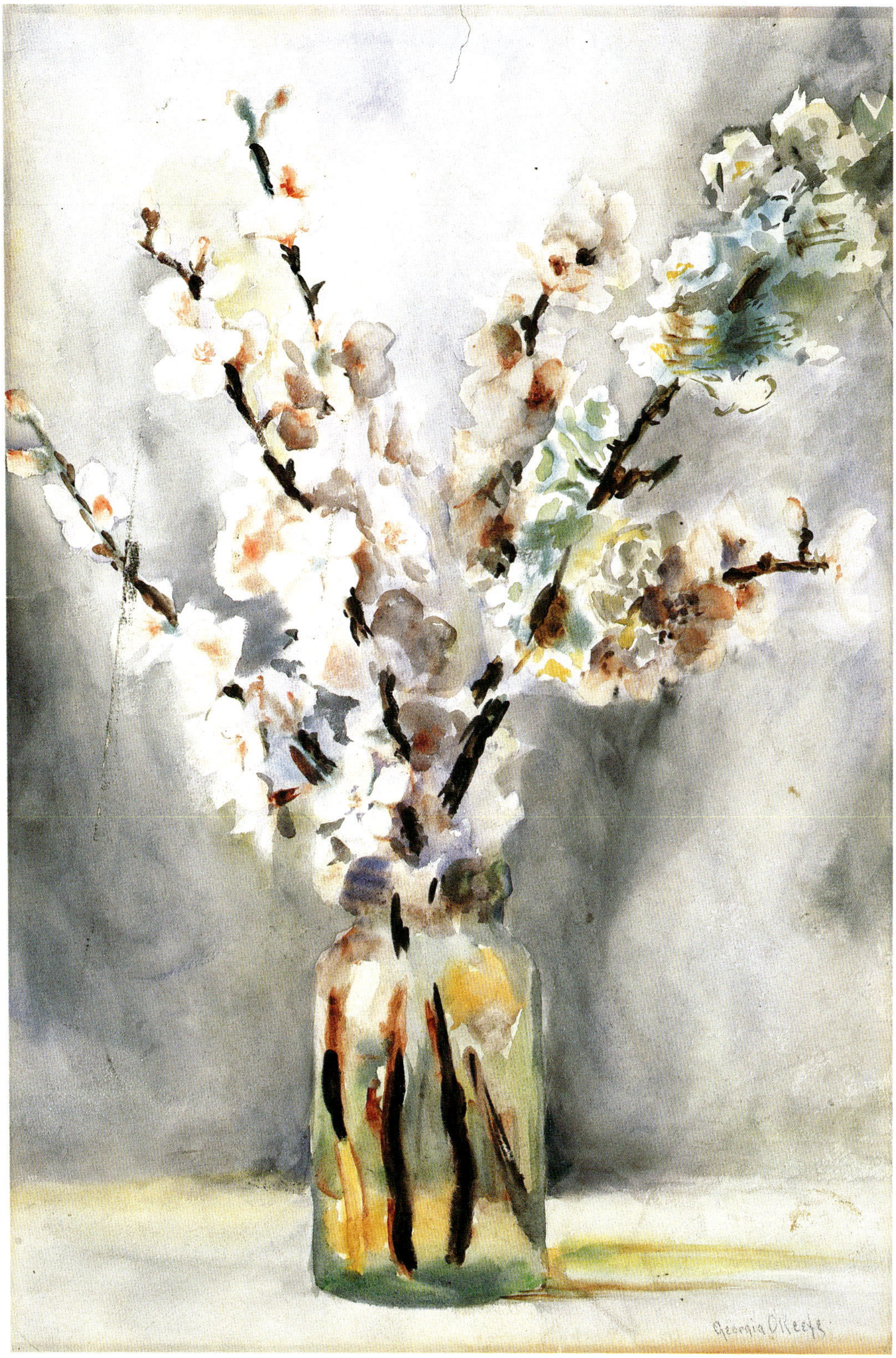
Georgia O'Keeffe

Plate 4. *Tent Door at Night*, ca. 1913, watercolor, 18-15/16 x 24-3/4 inches, University Art Museum, University of New Mexico, Albuquerque

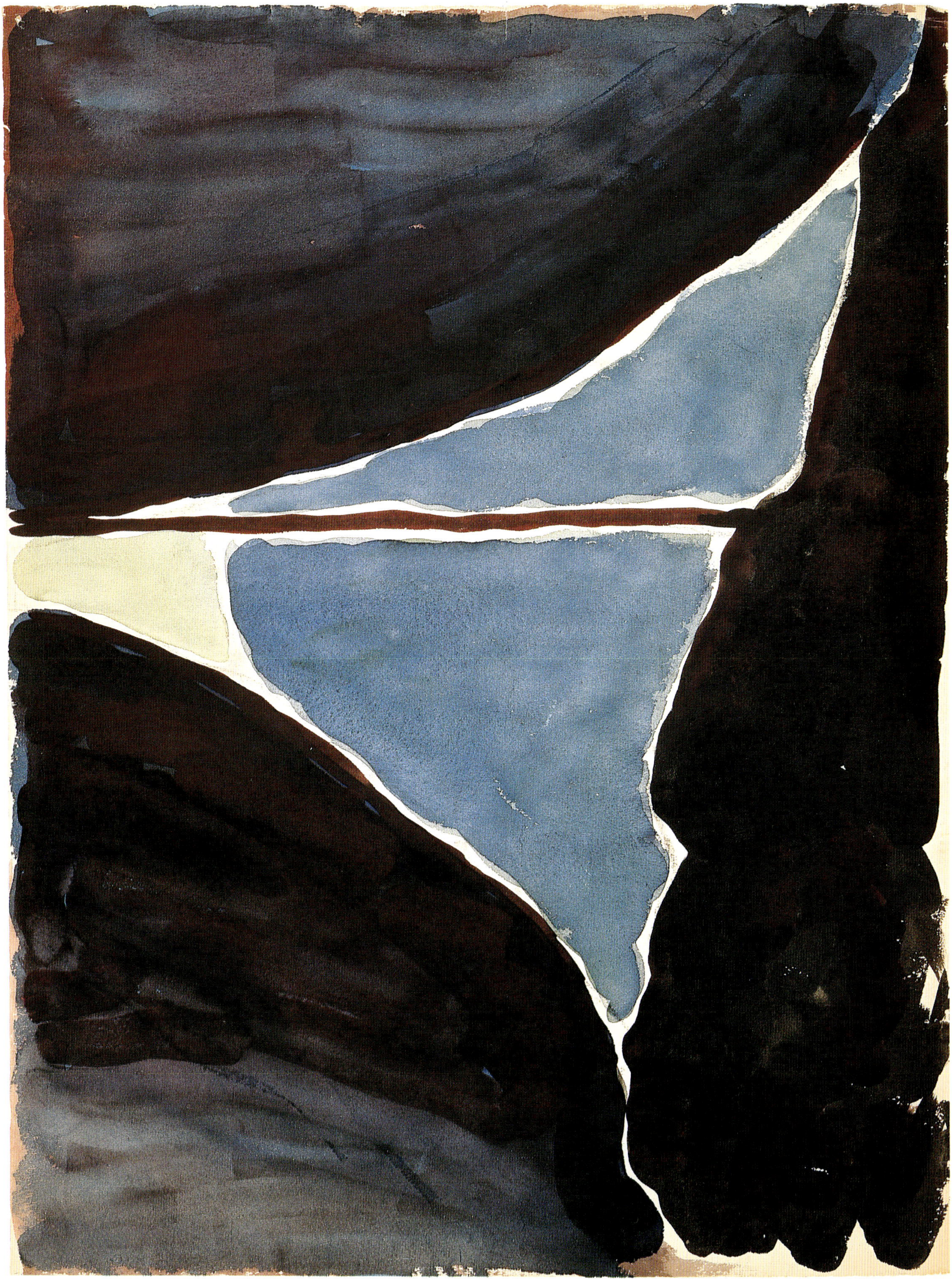

Plate 5. *Train at Night in the Desert*, 1916, charcoal, 24-3/4 x 19-1/4 inches, Anonymous loan

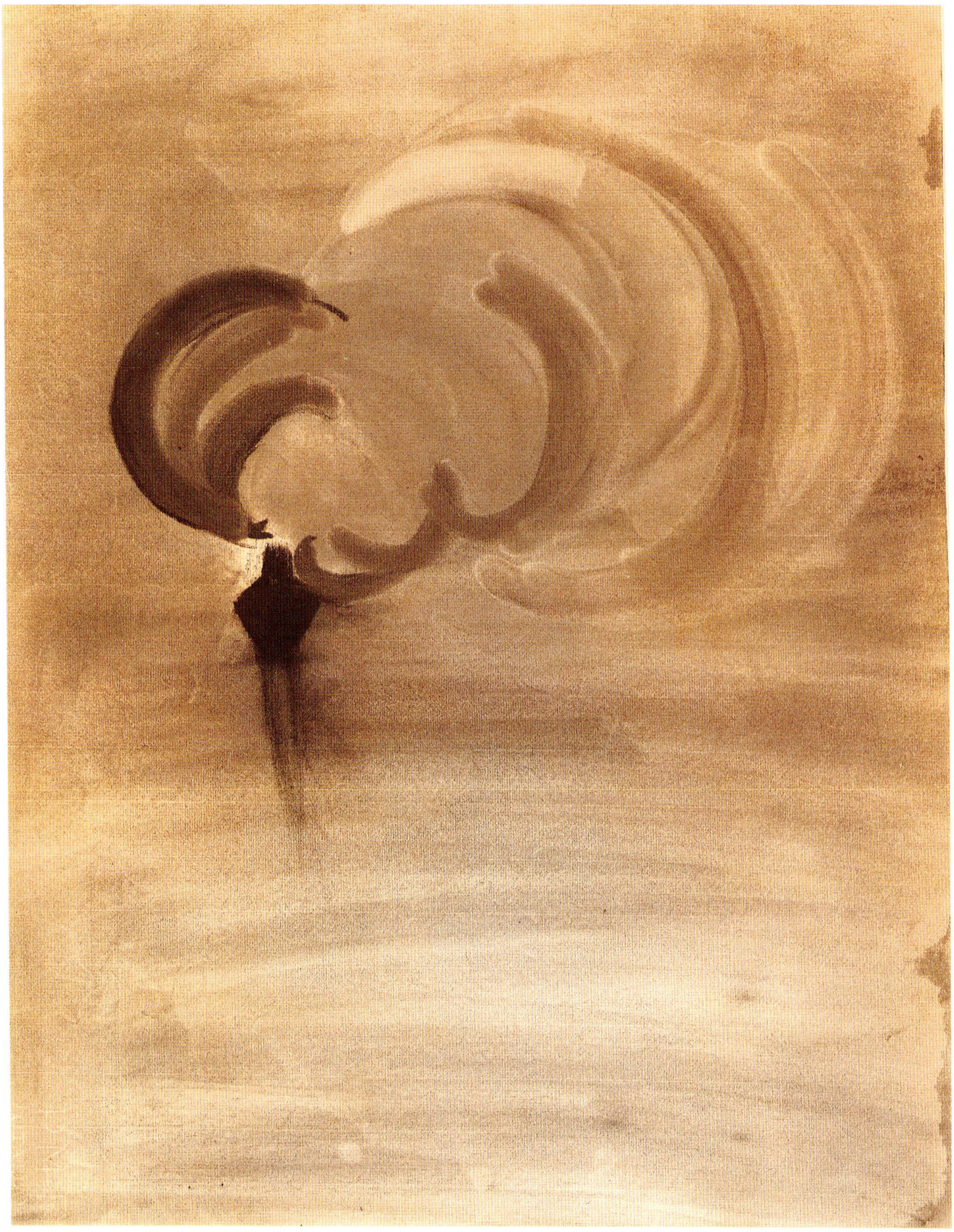

Plate 6. *Train at Night in the Desert*, 1916, watercolor, 12 x 8-7/8 inches, The Museum of Modern Art, New York. Acquired with matching funds from the Committee on Drawing and the National Endowment for the Arts.

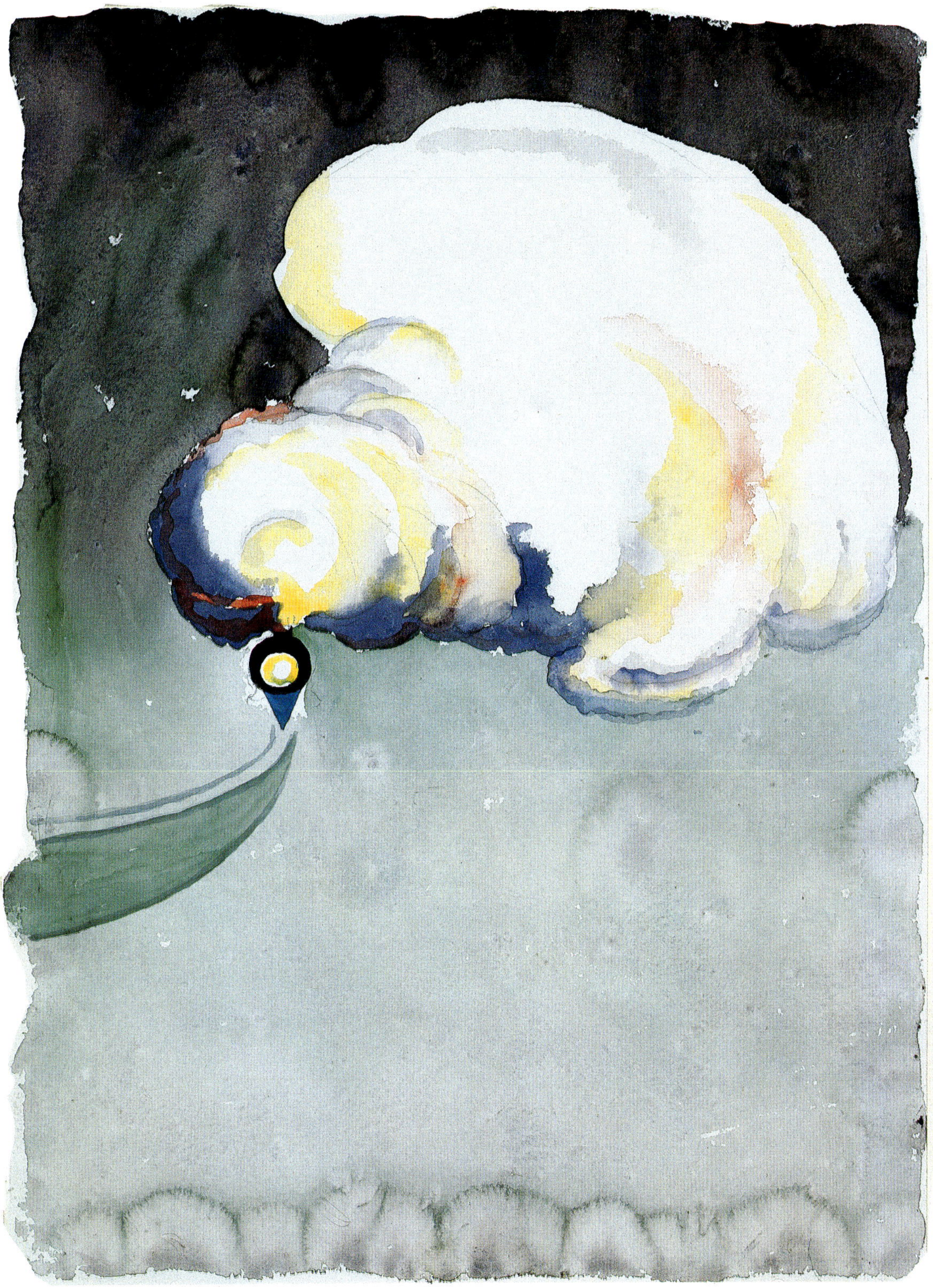

Plate 7. *Blue #4*, 1916, watercolor, 15-7/8 x 10-15/16 inches, The Brooklyn Museum, Bequest of Mary T. Cockcroft

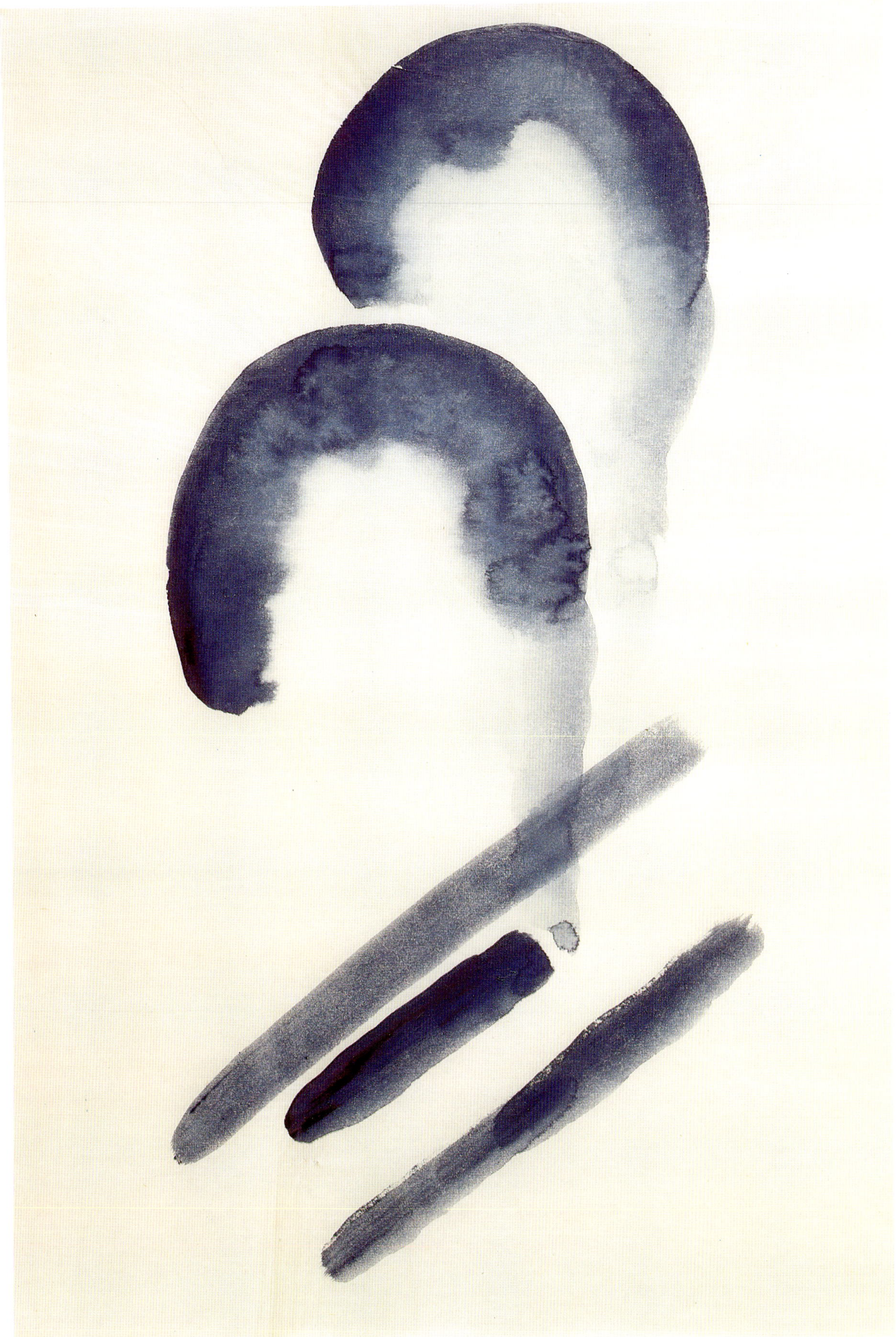

Plate 8. *Blue* I, ca. 1917, watercolor, 30-3/4 x 22-3/8 inches, Collection of Robert L. B. Tobin

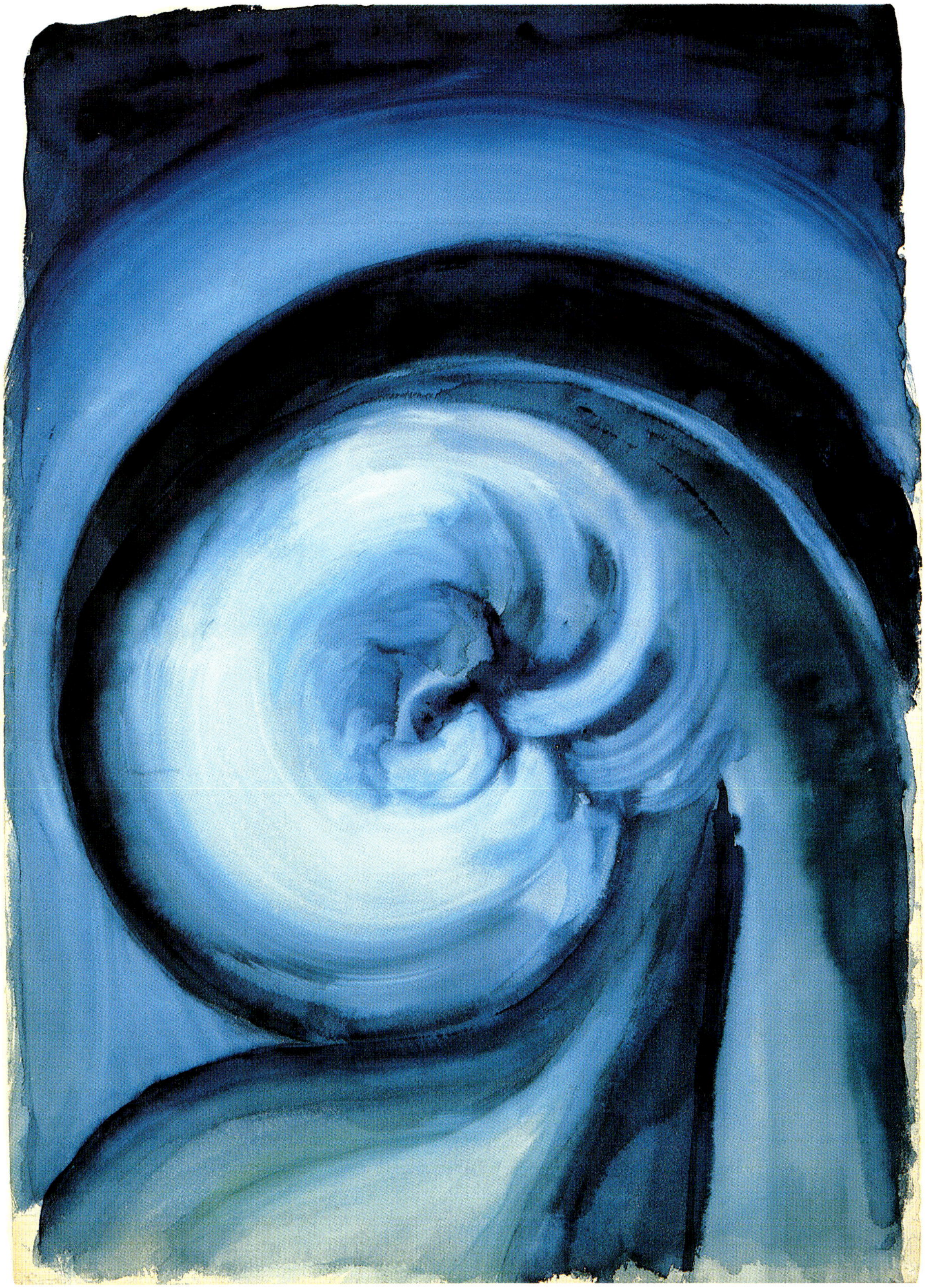

Plate 9. *Abstraction*, 1917, watercolor, 15-3/4 x 10-7/8 inches, Collection of Mr. and Mrs. Gerald P. Peters

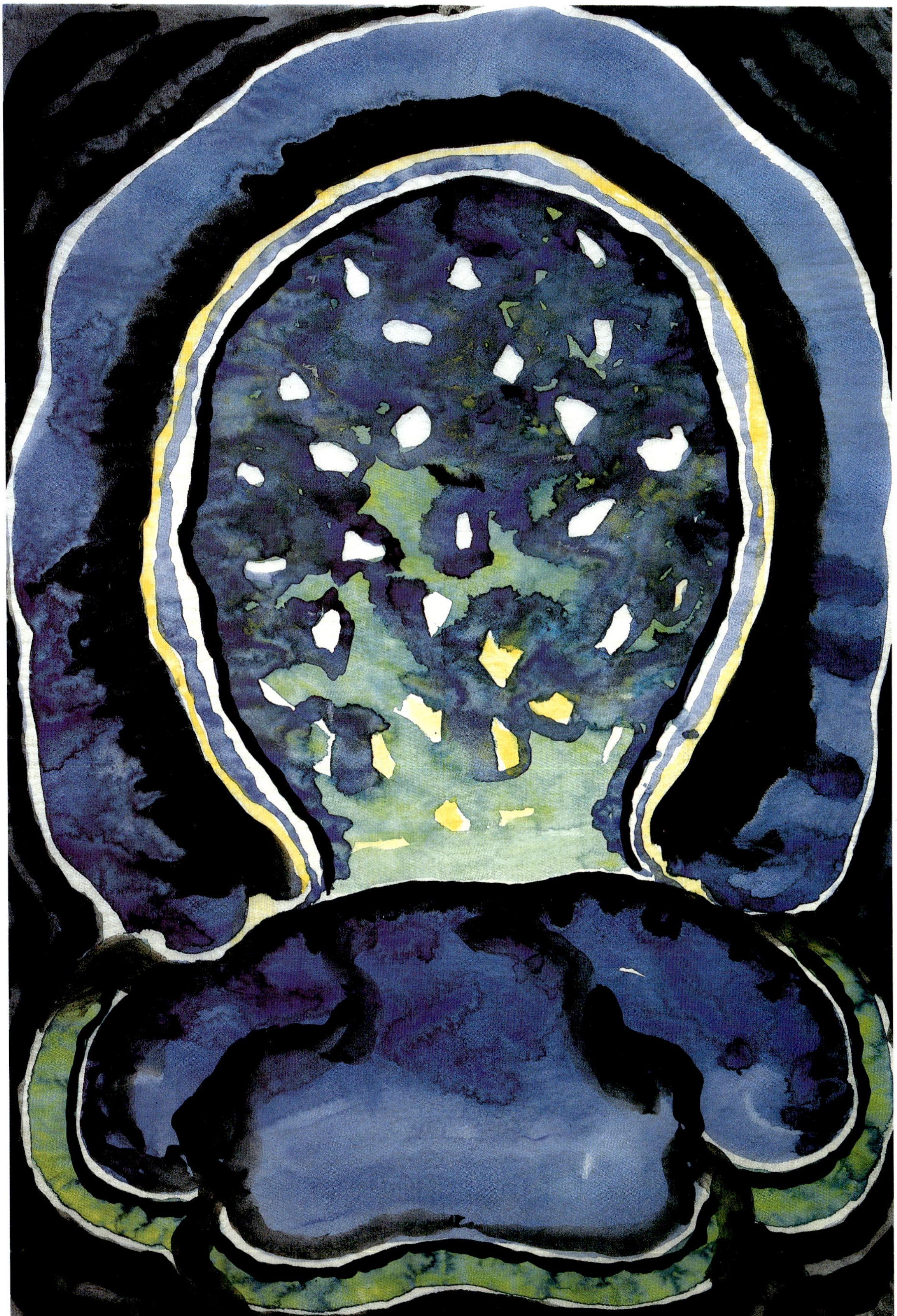

Plate 10. ***Red, Blue, and Green***, ca. 1916, watercolor, 17-1/2 x 13 inches, Courtesy of Washburn Gallery, New York

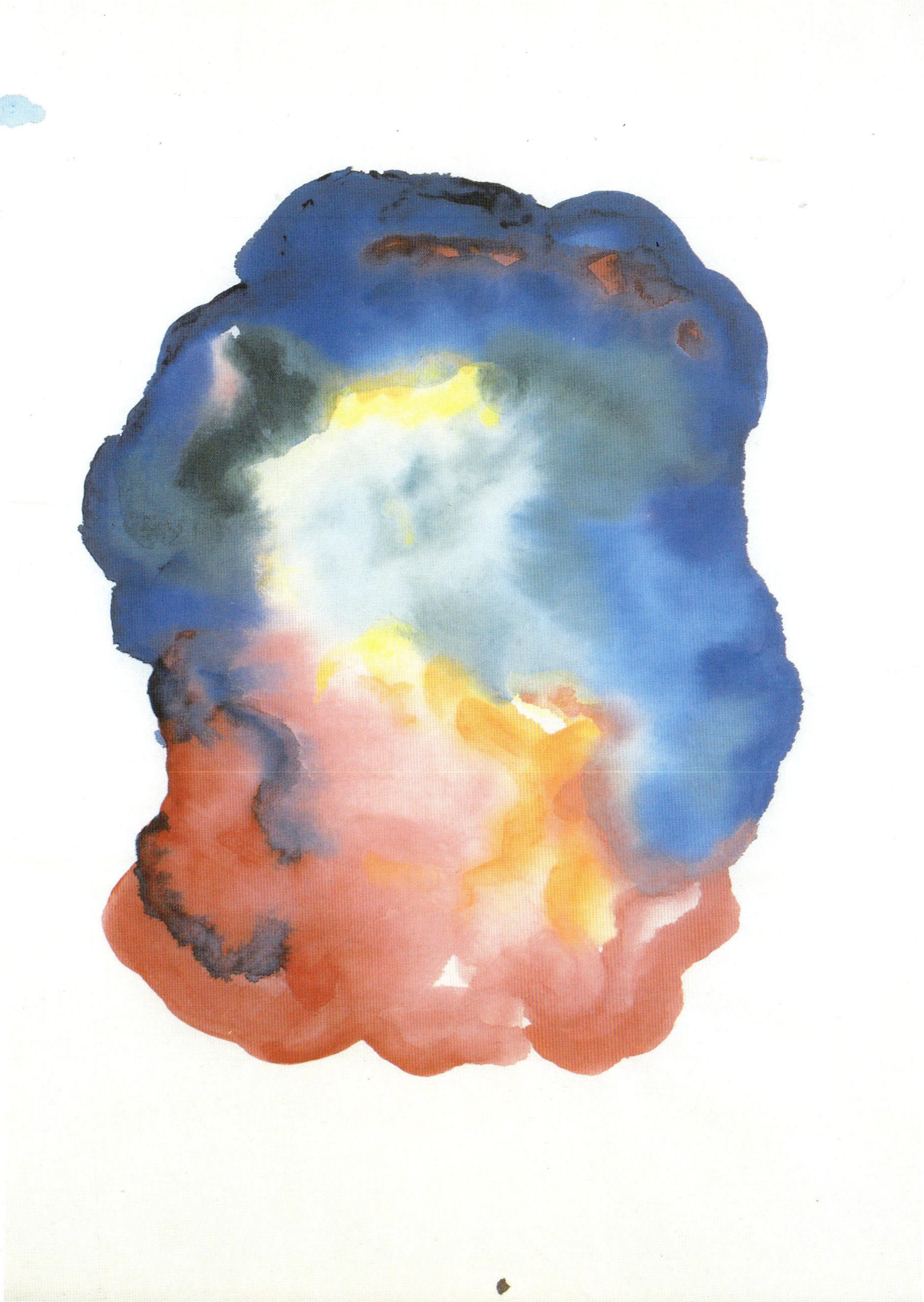

Plate 11. *Blue Hill #2*, ca. 1916, watercolor, 8-3/4 x 11-3/4 inches, Anonymous loan through the Columbus Museum of Art, Ohio

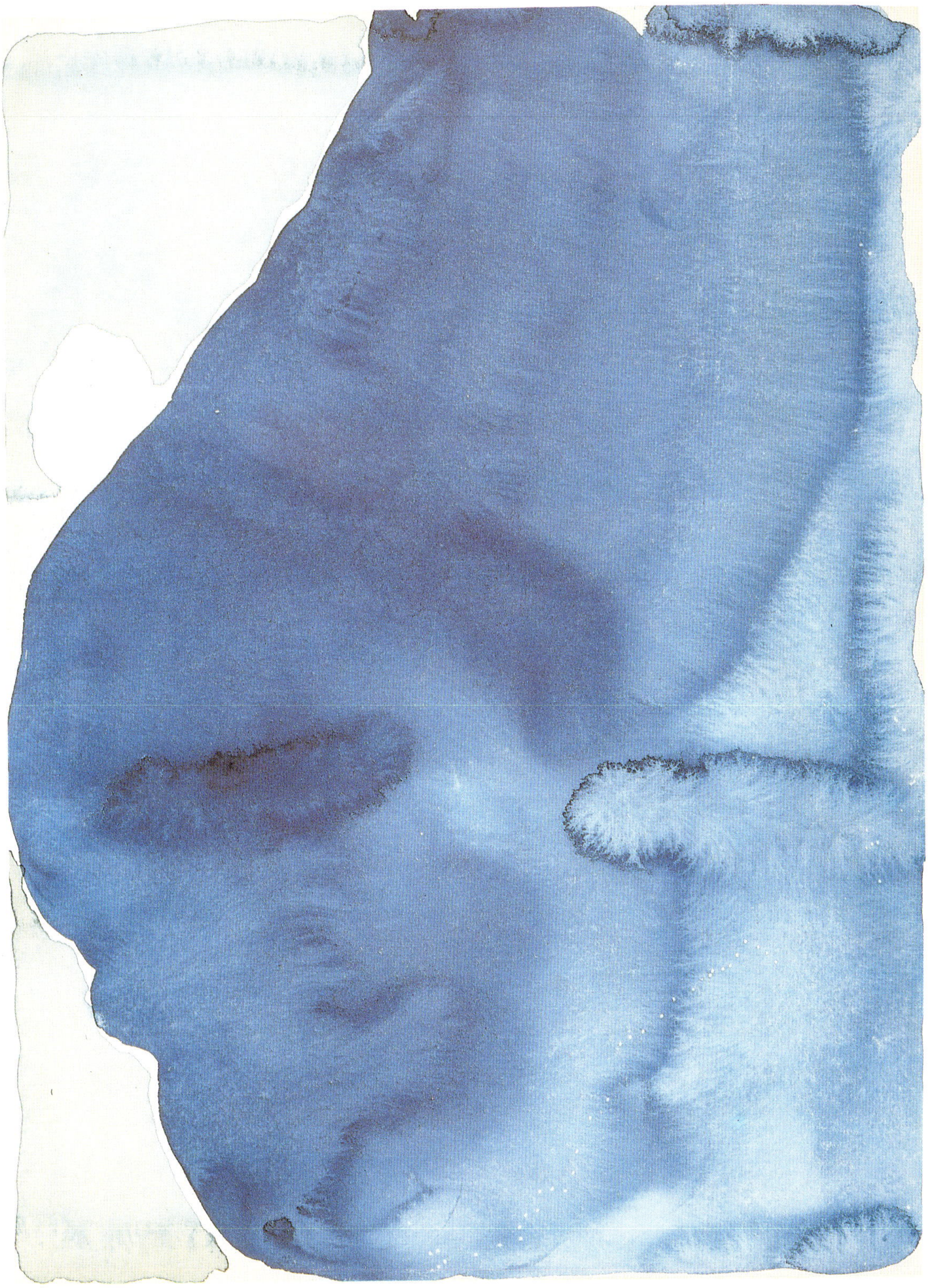

Plate 12. *Pink and Green Mountain*, No. 1, 1917, watercolor, 8-7/8 x 11-7/8 inches, The Helen Foresman Spencer Museum of Art, Museum Purchase: Letha Churchill Walker Fund

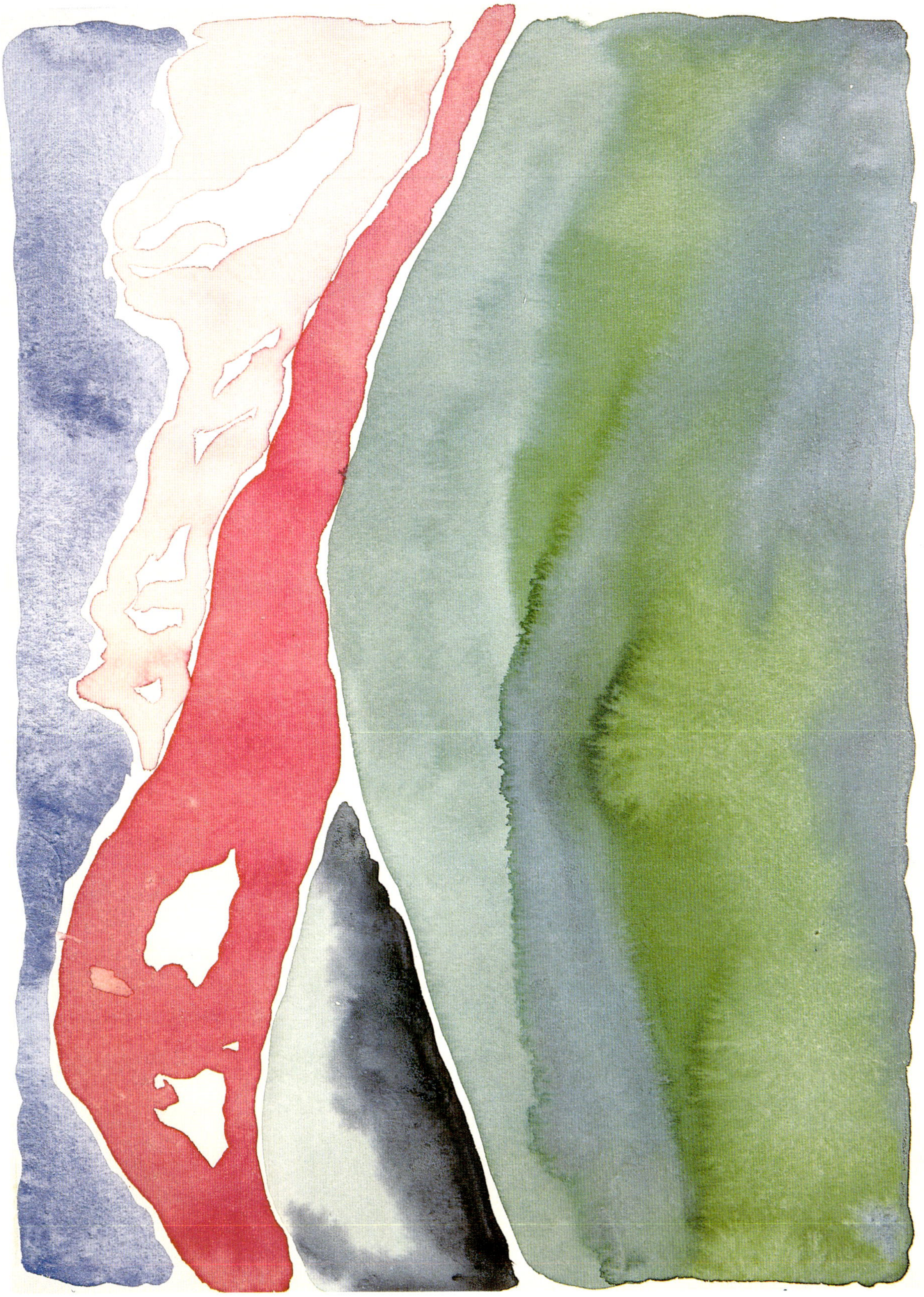

Plate 13. *Landscape and Layered Mountain*, 1917, watercolor, 8-7/8 x 12 inches, Collection of Mr. and Mrs. Warren Adelson

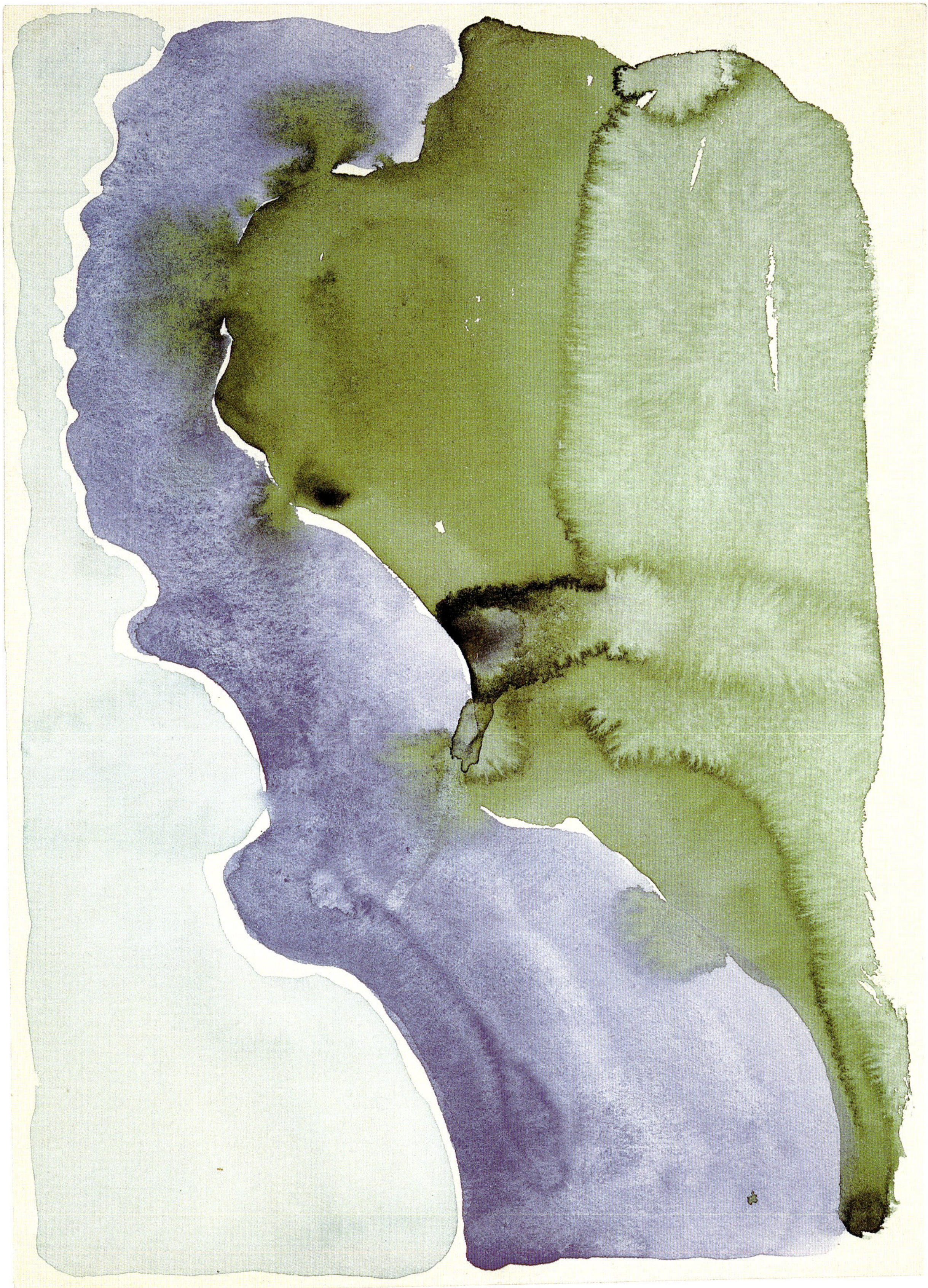

Plate 14. *Portrait W, No. 1*, 1917, watercolor, 9 x 12 inches, Courtesy of Sid Deutsch Gallery, New York

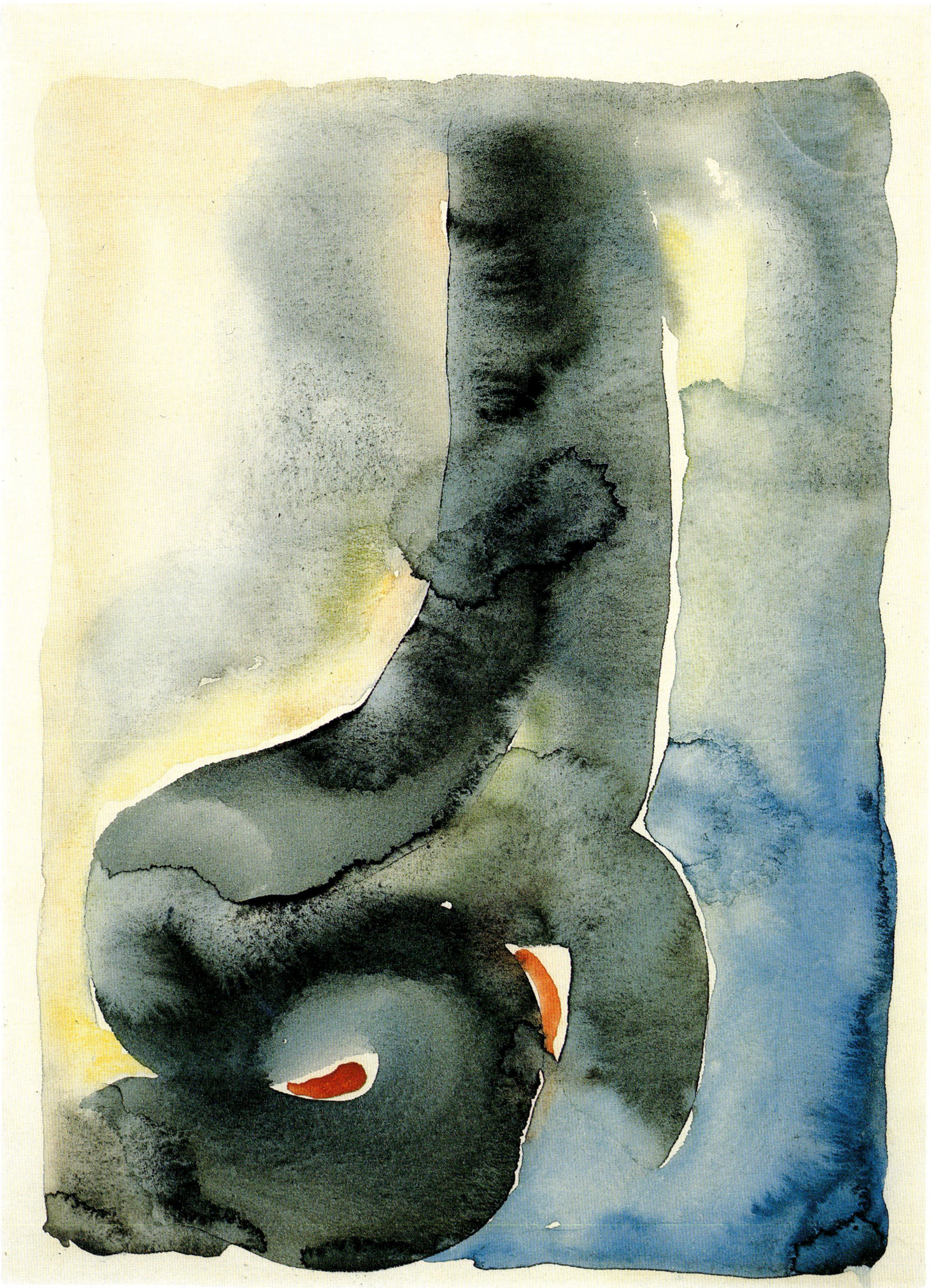

Plate 15. *Seated Nude* X1, 1917, watercolor, 11-7/8 x 8-7/8 inches, The Metropolitan Museum of Art, Purchase, Mr. and Mrs. Milton Petrie Gift, 1981

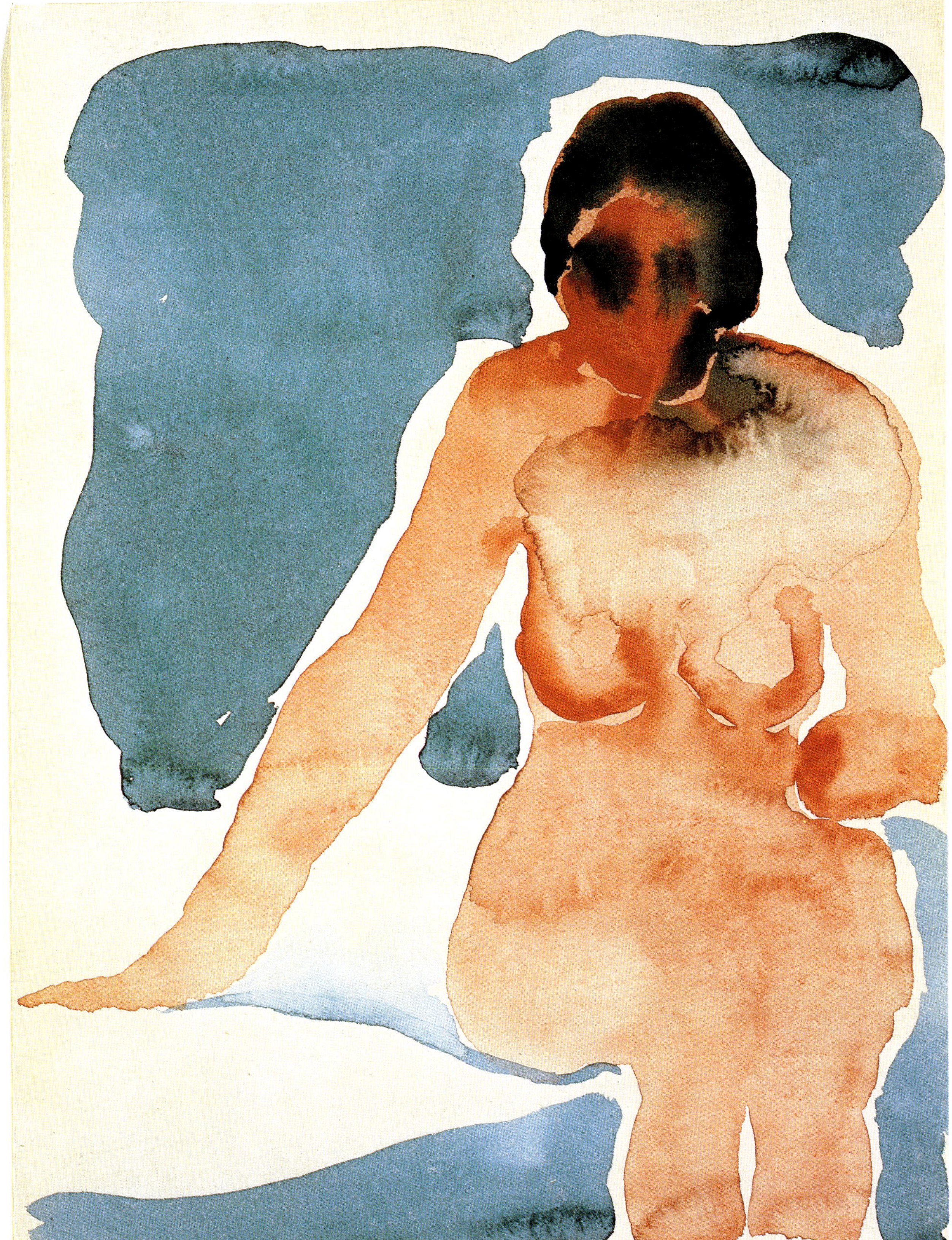

Plate 16. *Trees*, 1917, watercolor, 19 x 14-1/2 inches, Collection of Mark Carliner

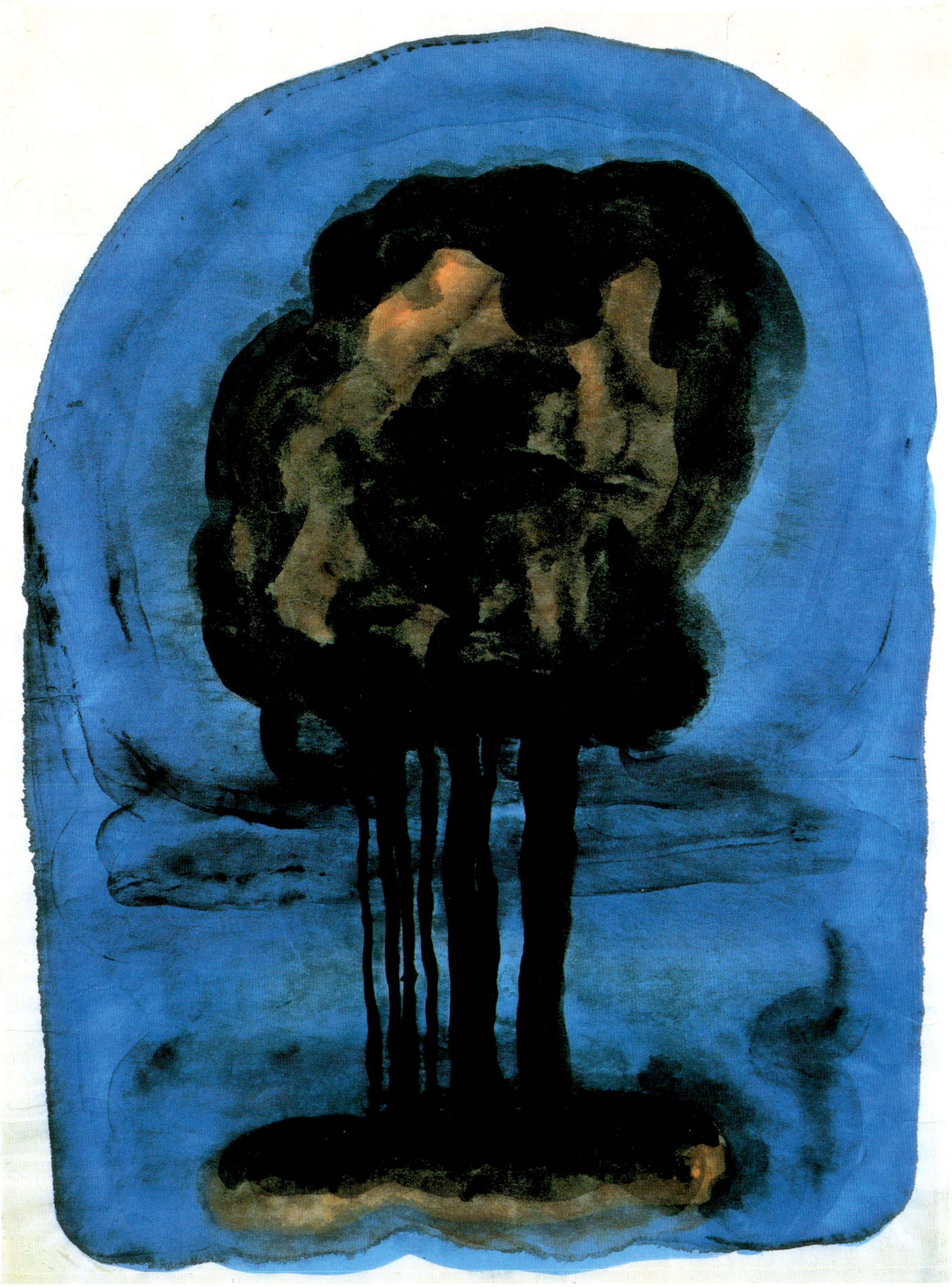

Plate 17. ***The Flag***, 1918, watercolor, 11-7/8 x 8-3/4 inches, Milwaukee Art Museum, Gift of Mrs. Harry Lynde Bradley

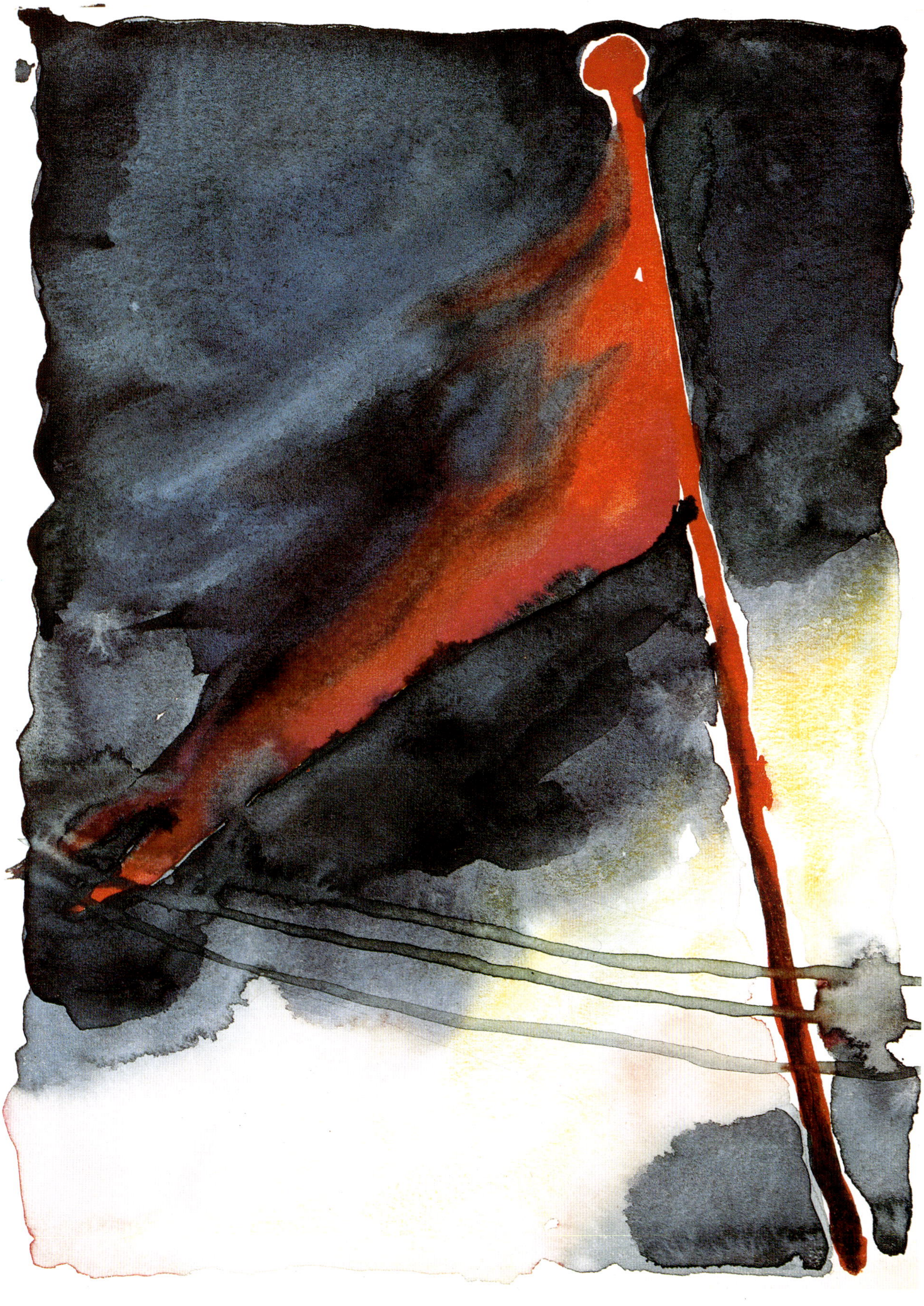

Plate 18. *Evening Star* No. II, 1917, watercolor, 9 x 12 inches, Anonymous loan

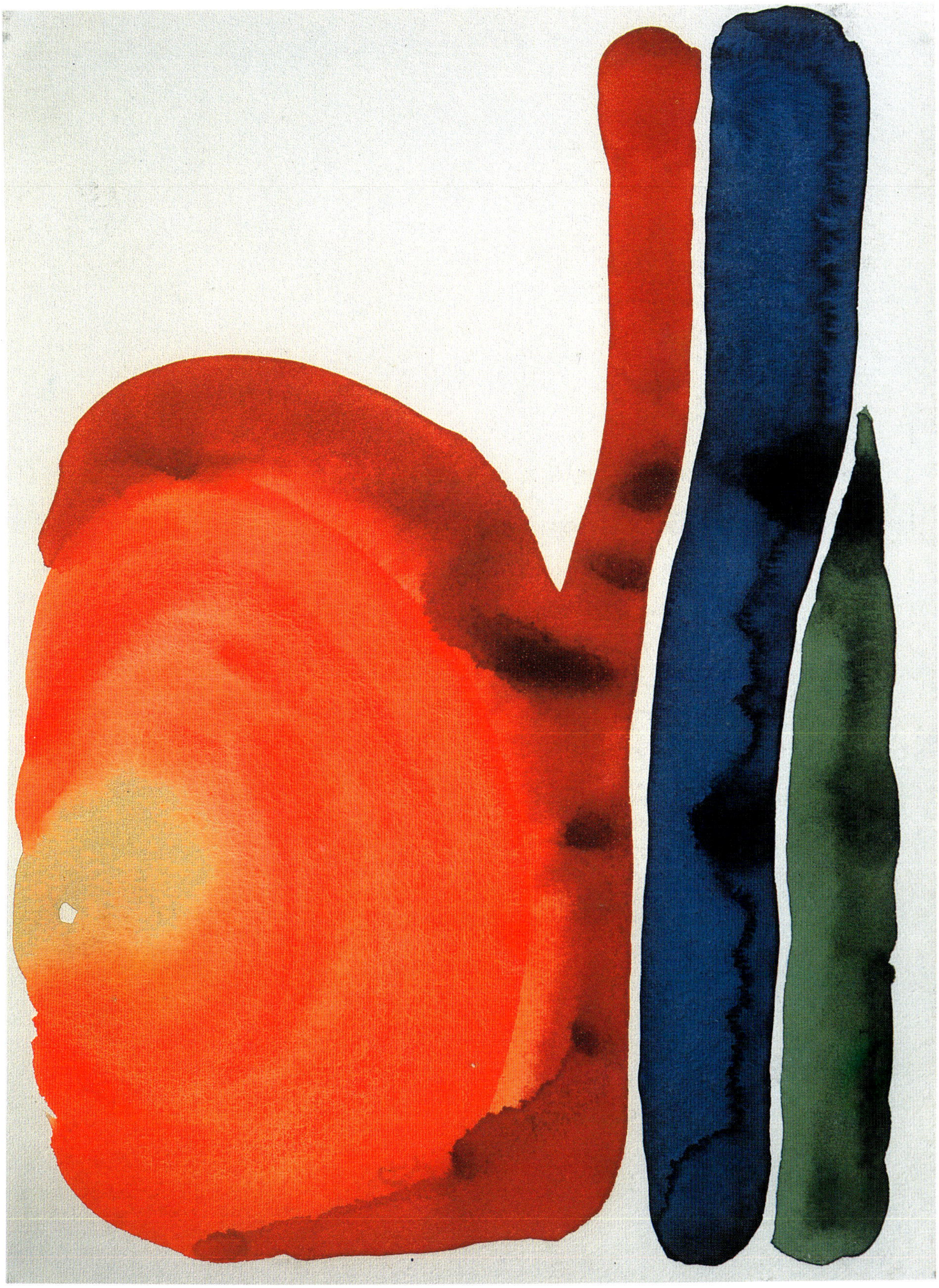

Plate 19. *Evening Star* No. III, 1917, watercolor, 9 x 12 inches, The Museum of Modern Art, Mr. and Mrs. Donald B. Straus Fund

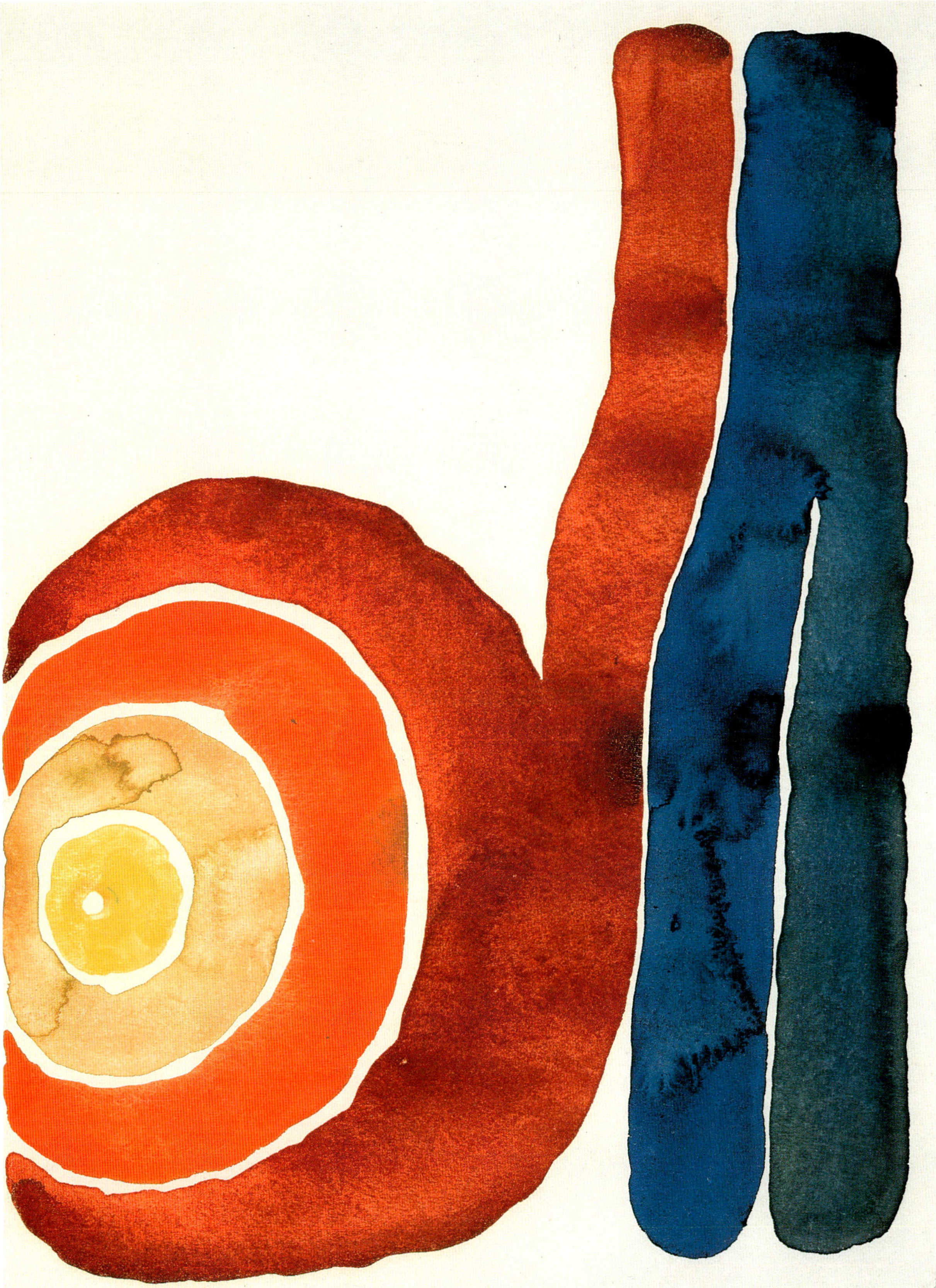

Plate 20. *Evening Star* No. V, 1917, watercolor, 9 x 12 inches, Anonymous loan

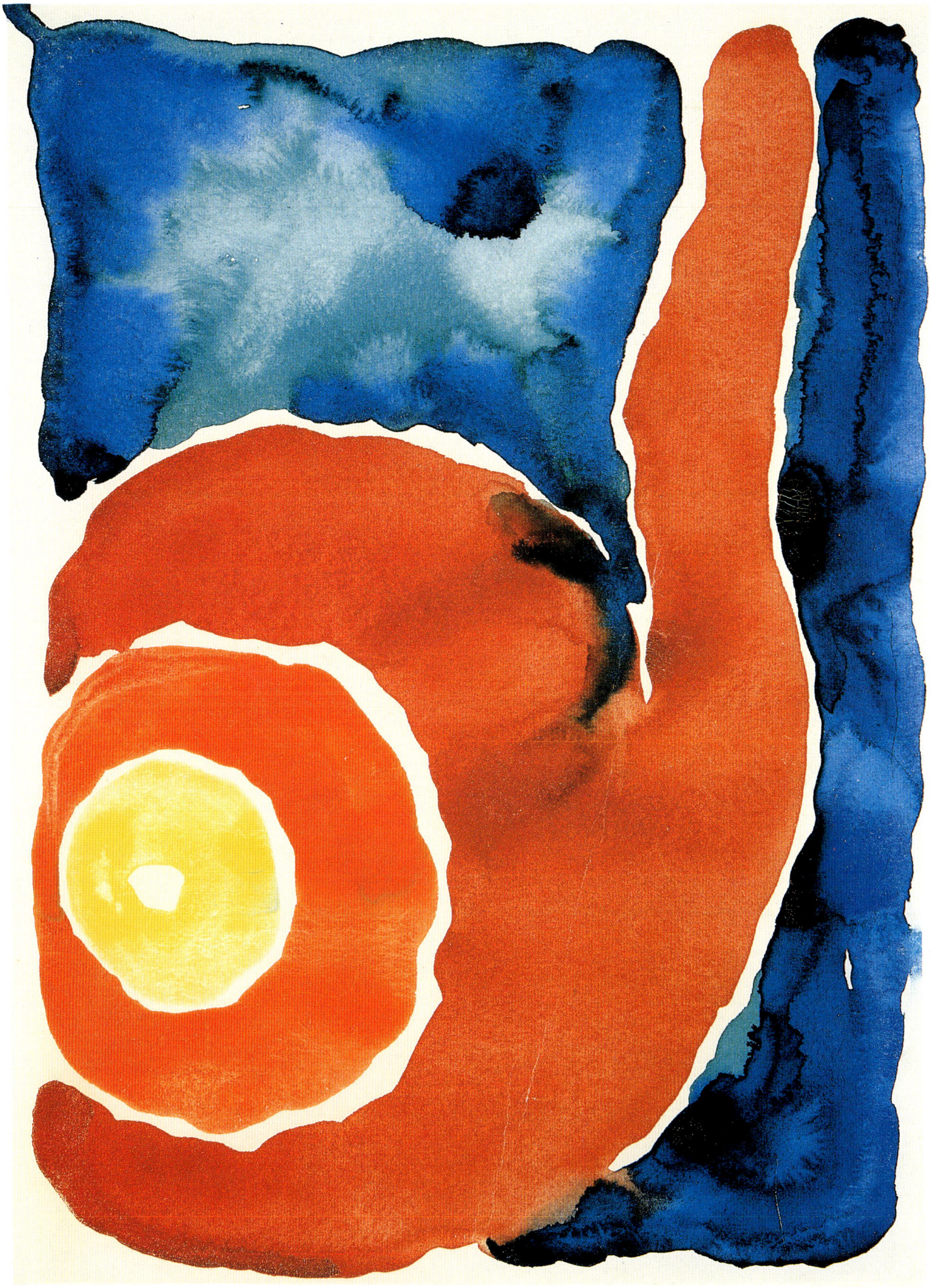

Plate 21. *Evening Star No. VII*, 1917, watercolor, 9 x 12 inches, Collection of Dore Previn

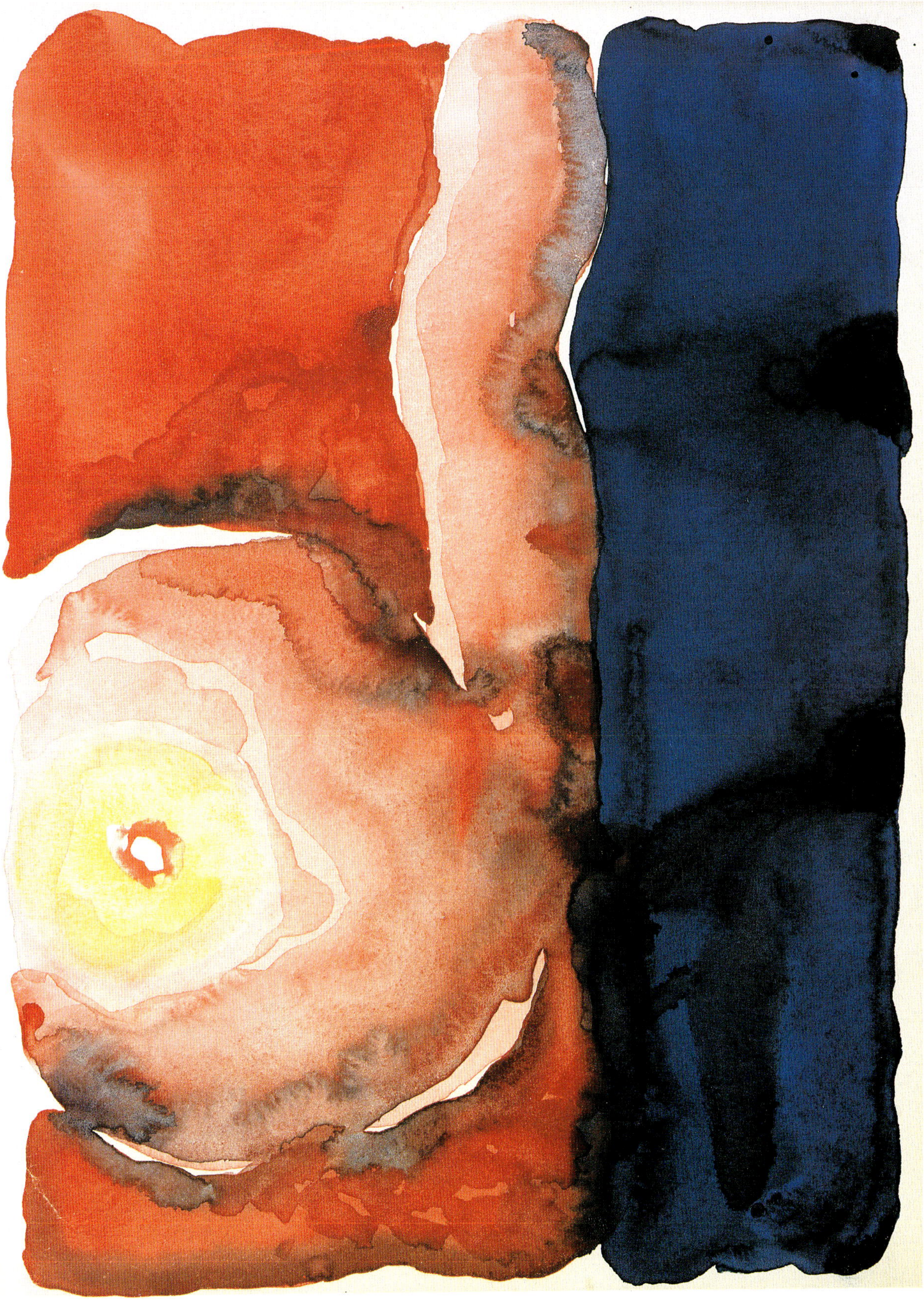

Plate 22. *Evening Star*, 1917, watercolor, 13-3/4 x 17-3/4 inches, Yale University Art Gallery

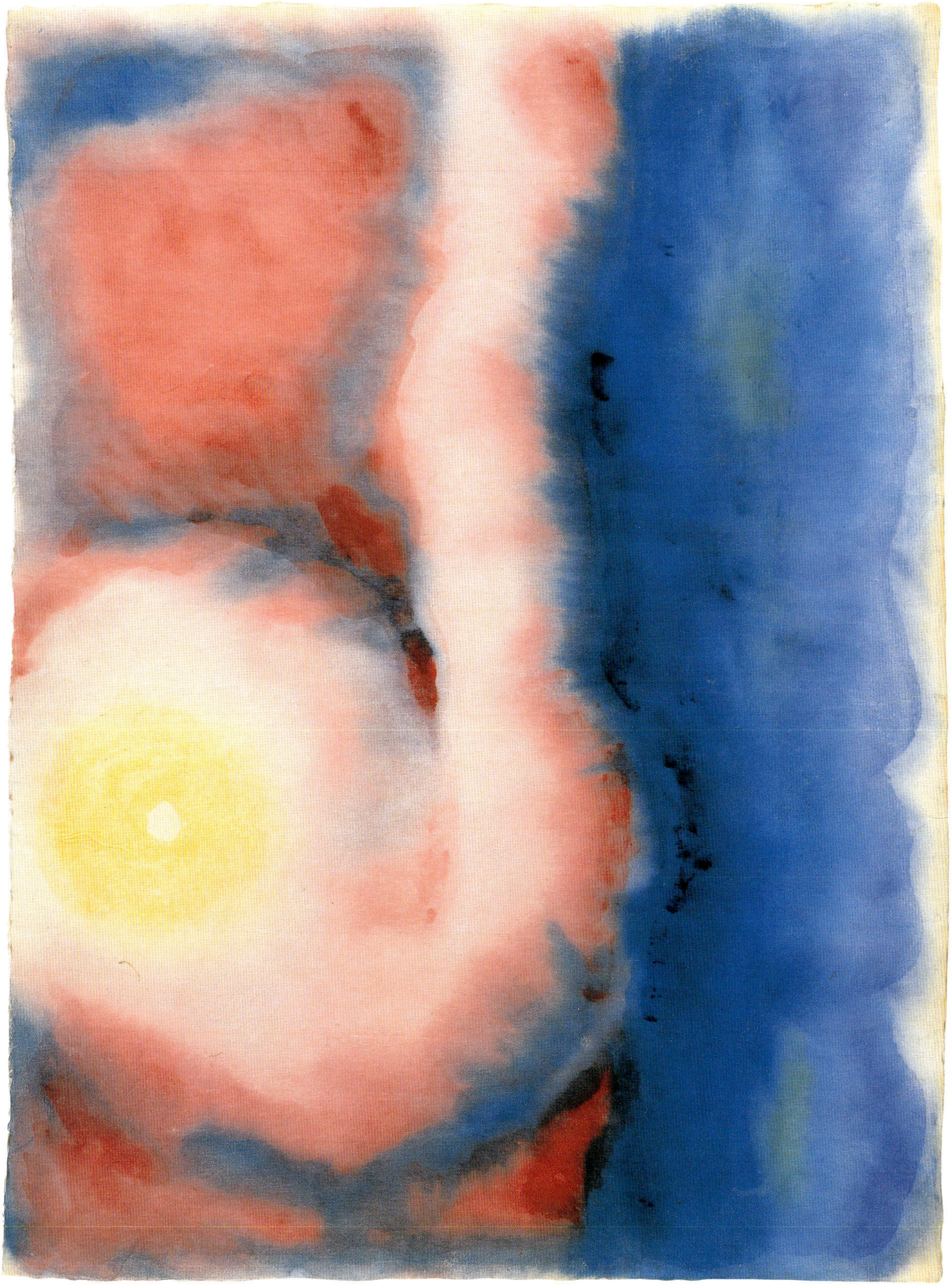

Plate 23. ***Canna Lily***, 1919, watercolor, 23 x 12-7/8 inches, Columbus Museum of Art, Museum Purchase: Derby Fund

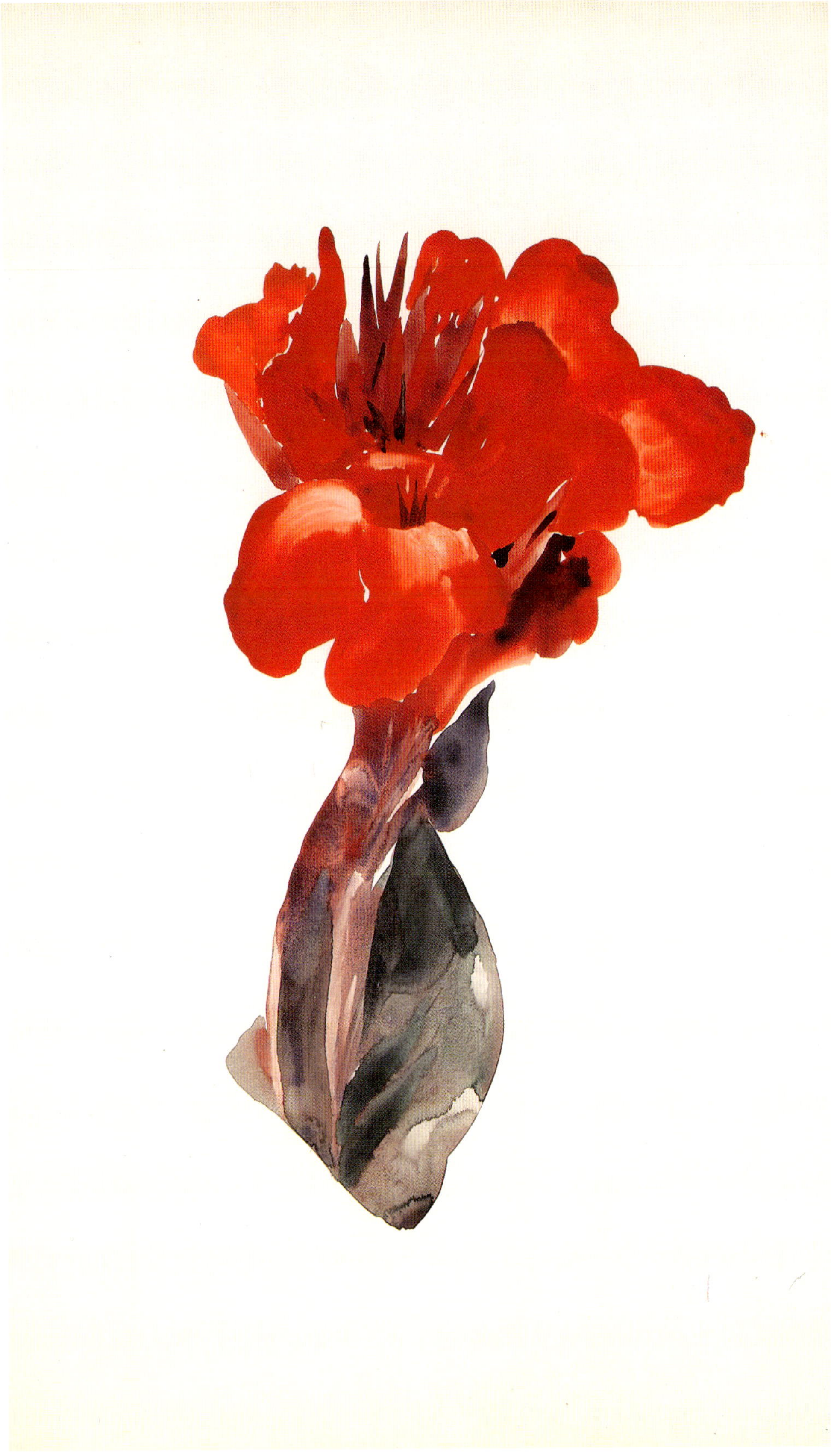

Plate 24. ***Red Canna***, ca. 1920, watercolor, 19-5/16 x 13 inches, Yale University Art Gallery

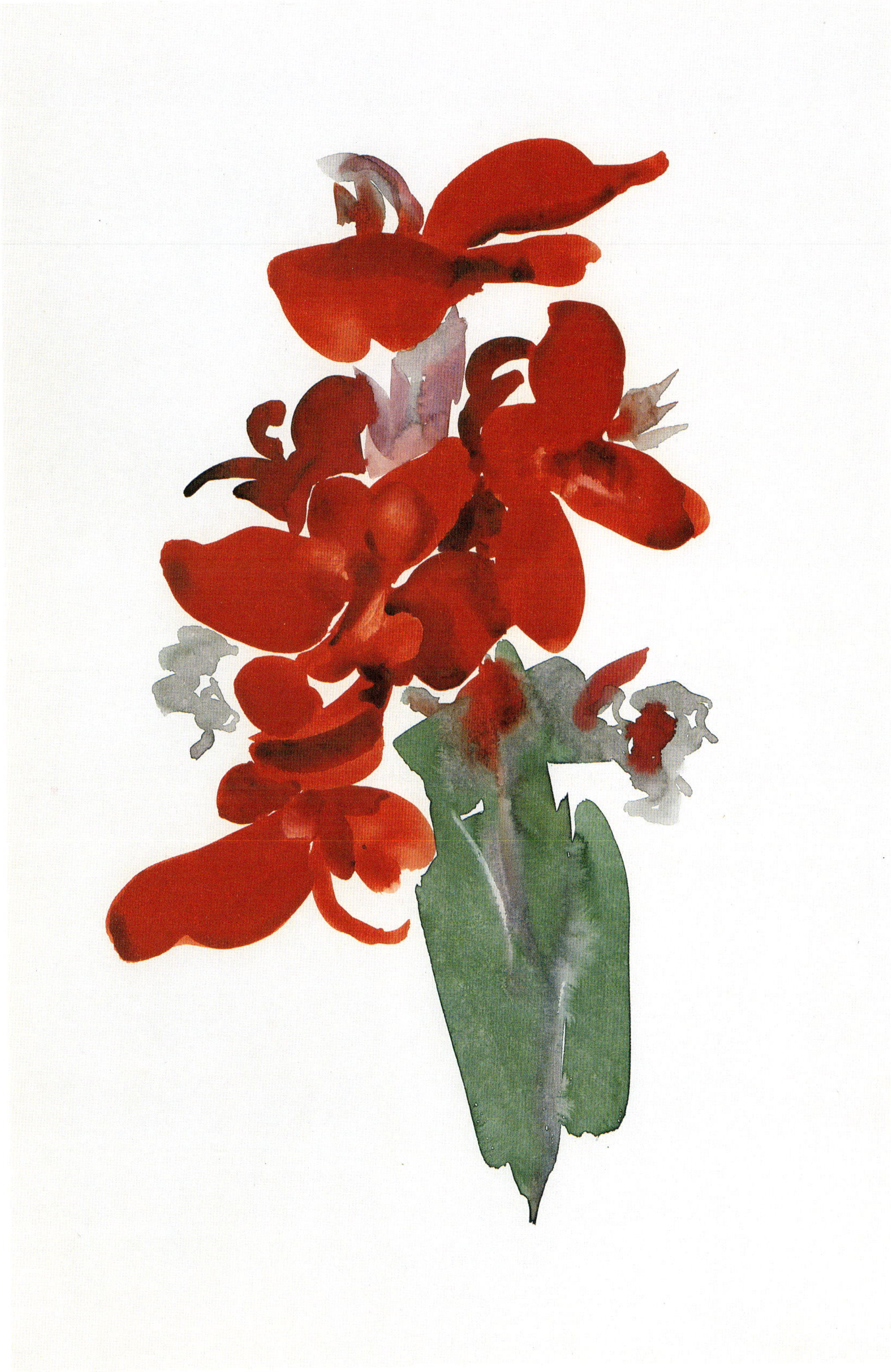

Plate 25. *Lake George and Woods*, ca. 1922, pastel, 16 x 13-3/4 inches, Collection of Mr. and Mrs. John Palmer Leeper

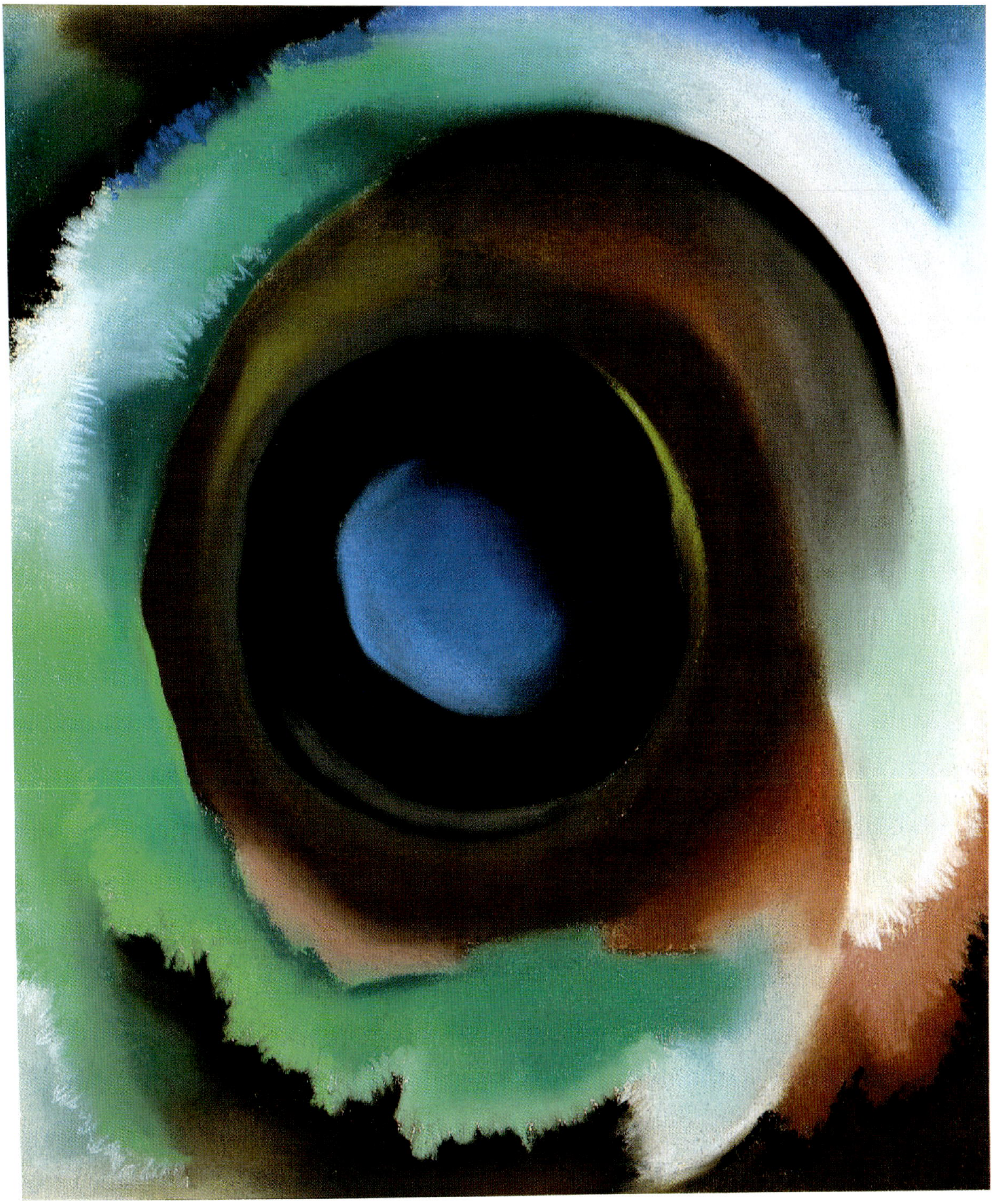

Plate 26. *Maine*, 1922, watercolor, 18 x 11 inches, Courtesy of Kennedy Galleries, New York

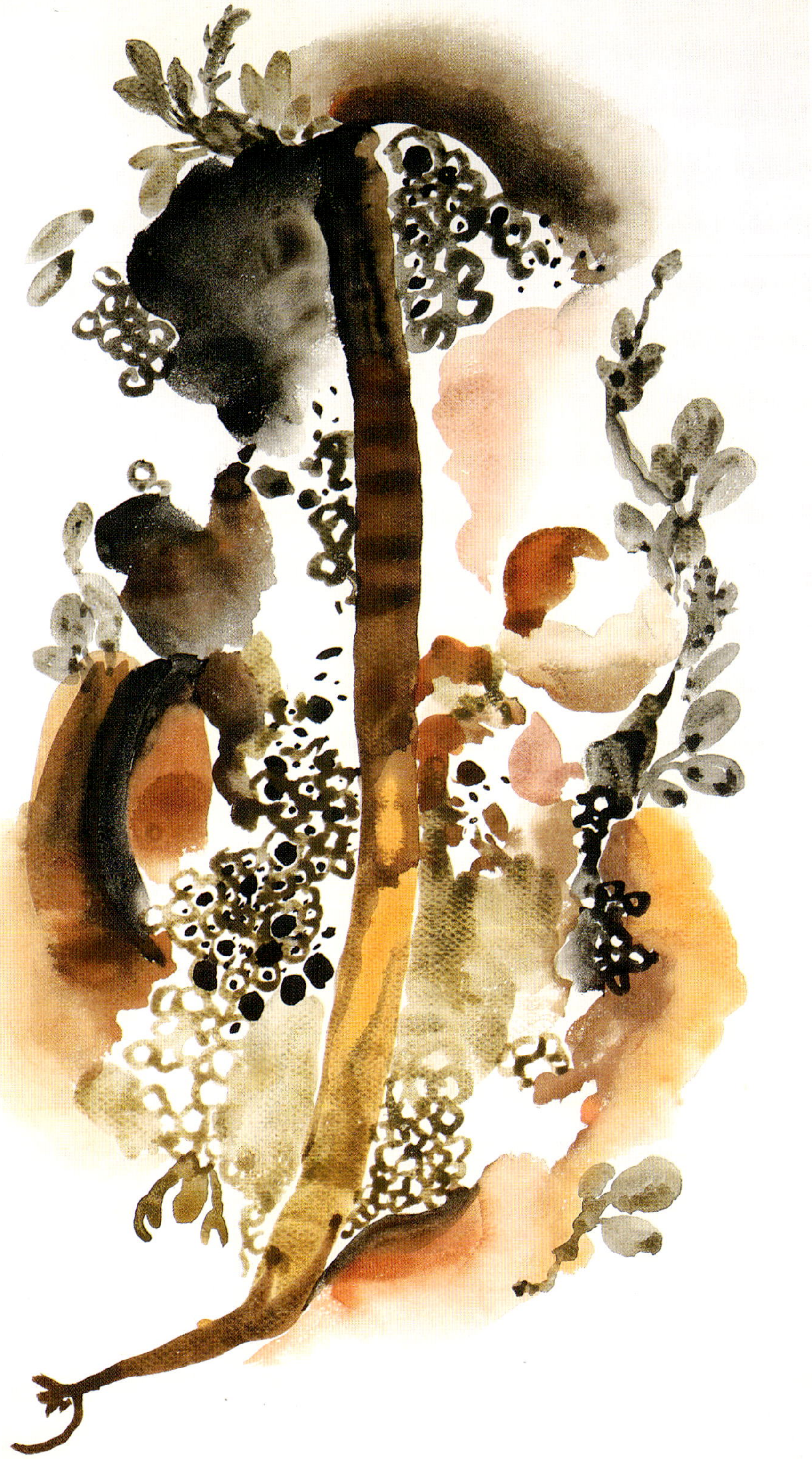

Plate 27. *New York Rooftops*, ca. 1925–30, charcoal, 24-1/2 x 18-3/4 inches, The Fine Arts Museums of San Francisco, Achenbach Foundation for Graphic Arts, Gift of Mrs. Charlotte S. Mack

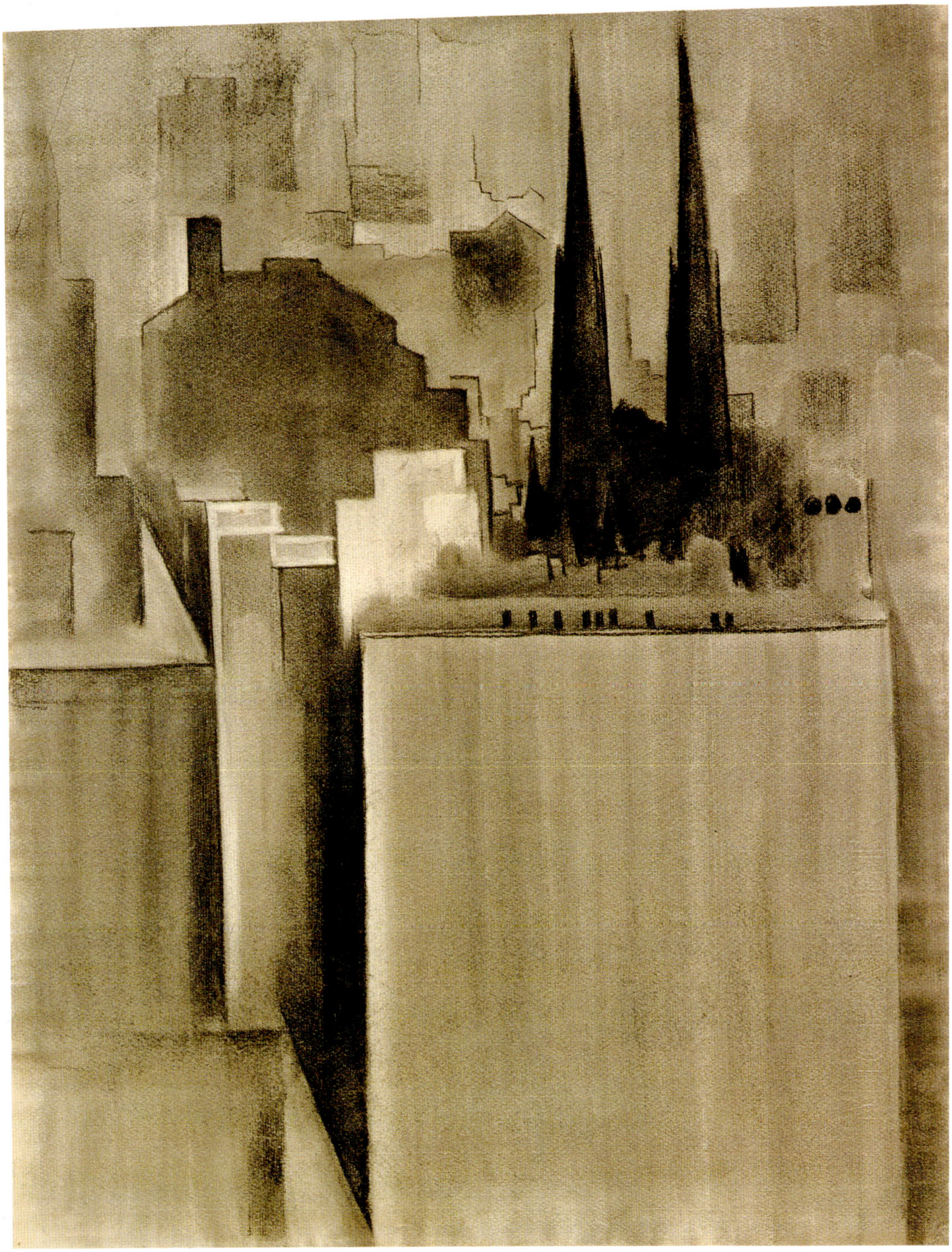

Plate 28. *East River with Sun*, 1926, pastel, 10-7/8 x 27-7/8 inches, Anonymous loan

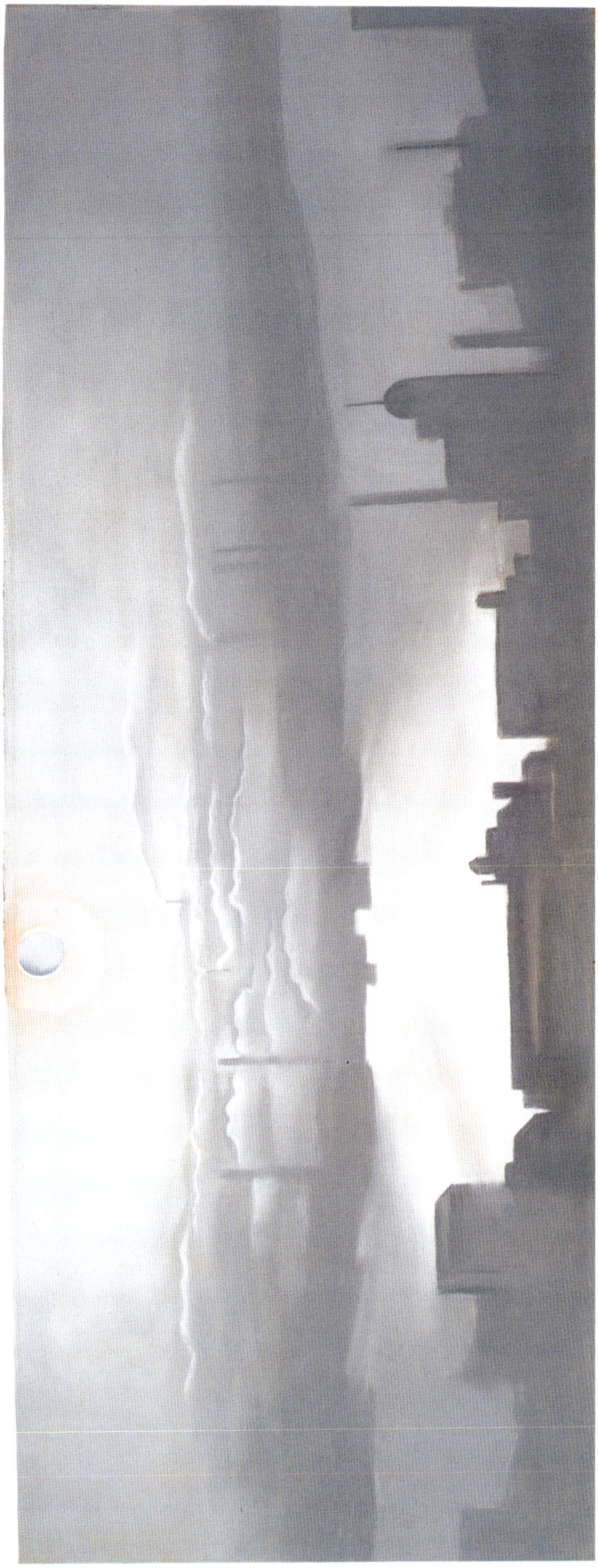

Plate 29. *Shell*, ca. 1928, charcoal, 18-11/16 x 24-3/4 inches, National Gallery of Art, Gift of Dorothy Edinburg

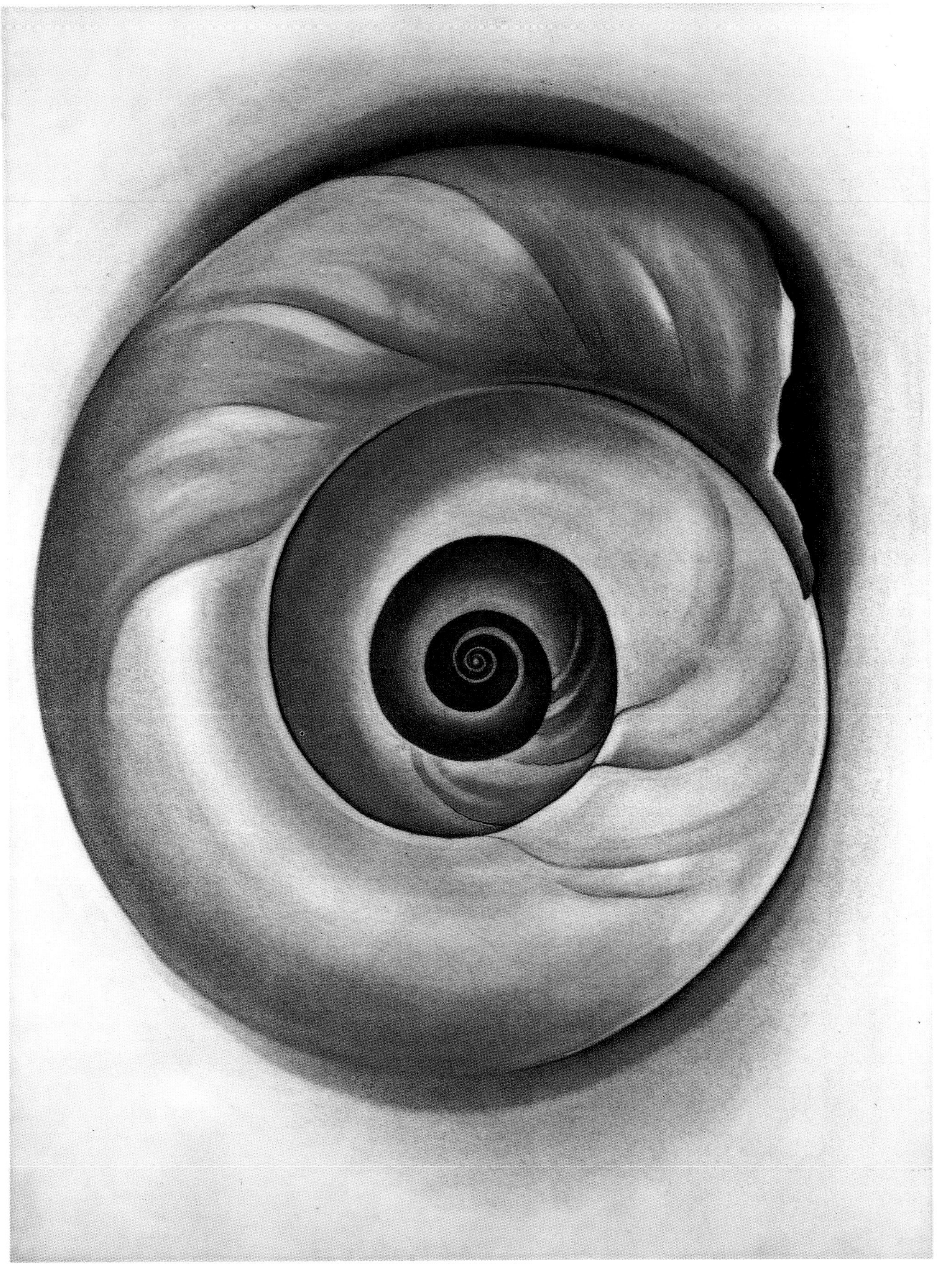

Plate 30. *Banyon Tree Trunk, Bermuda*, 1934, pencil, 21-3/4 x 14-3/4 inches, Courtesy of Hirschl and Adler Galleries, Inc., New York

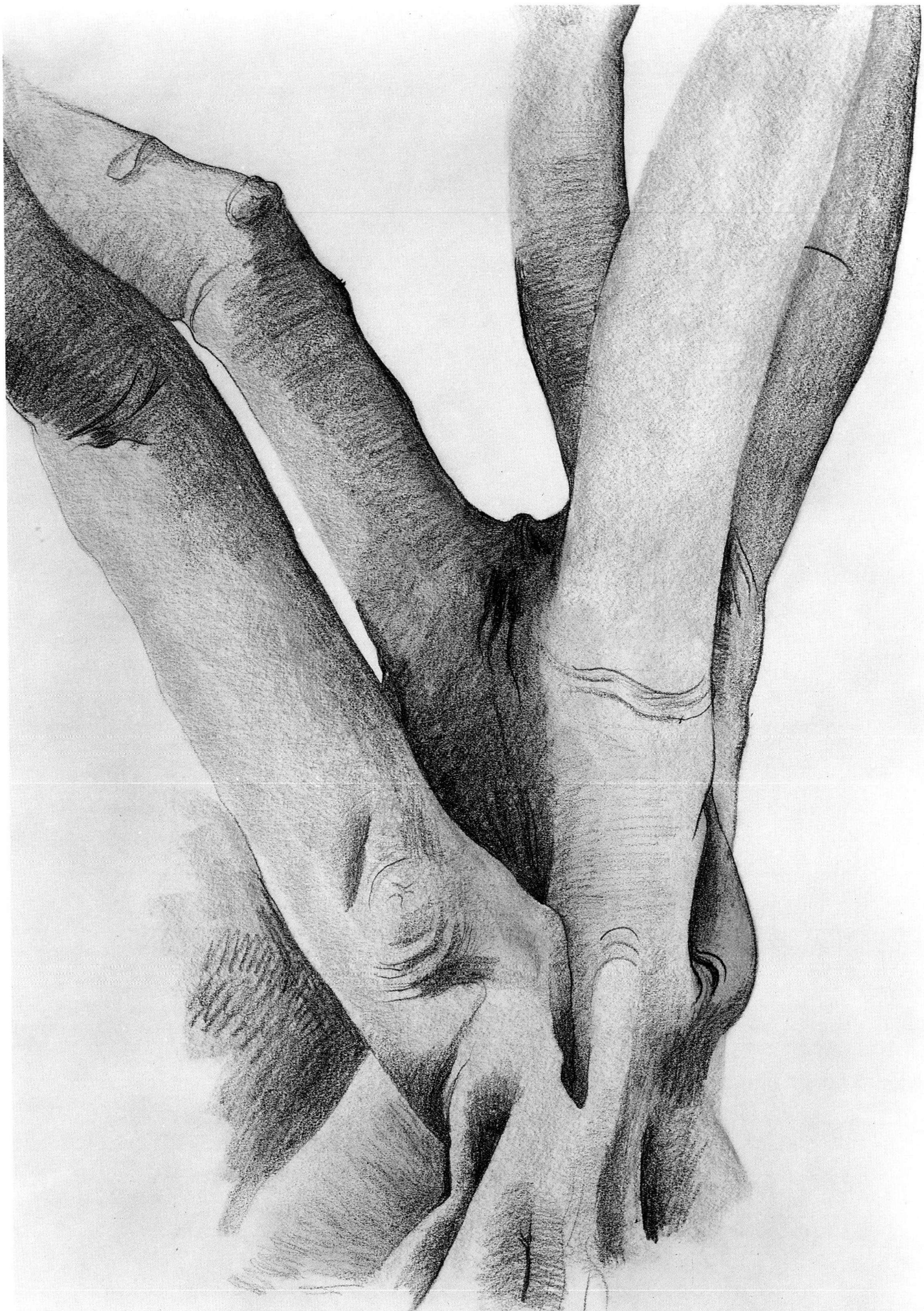

Plate 31. ***Blue-Headed Indian Doll***, 1935, watercolor, 20-1/2 x 11-1/2 inches, Collection of King Investments Co., Dallas, Texas

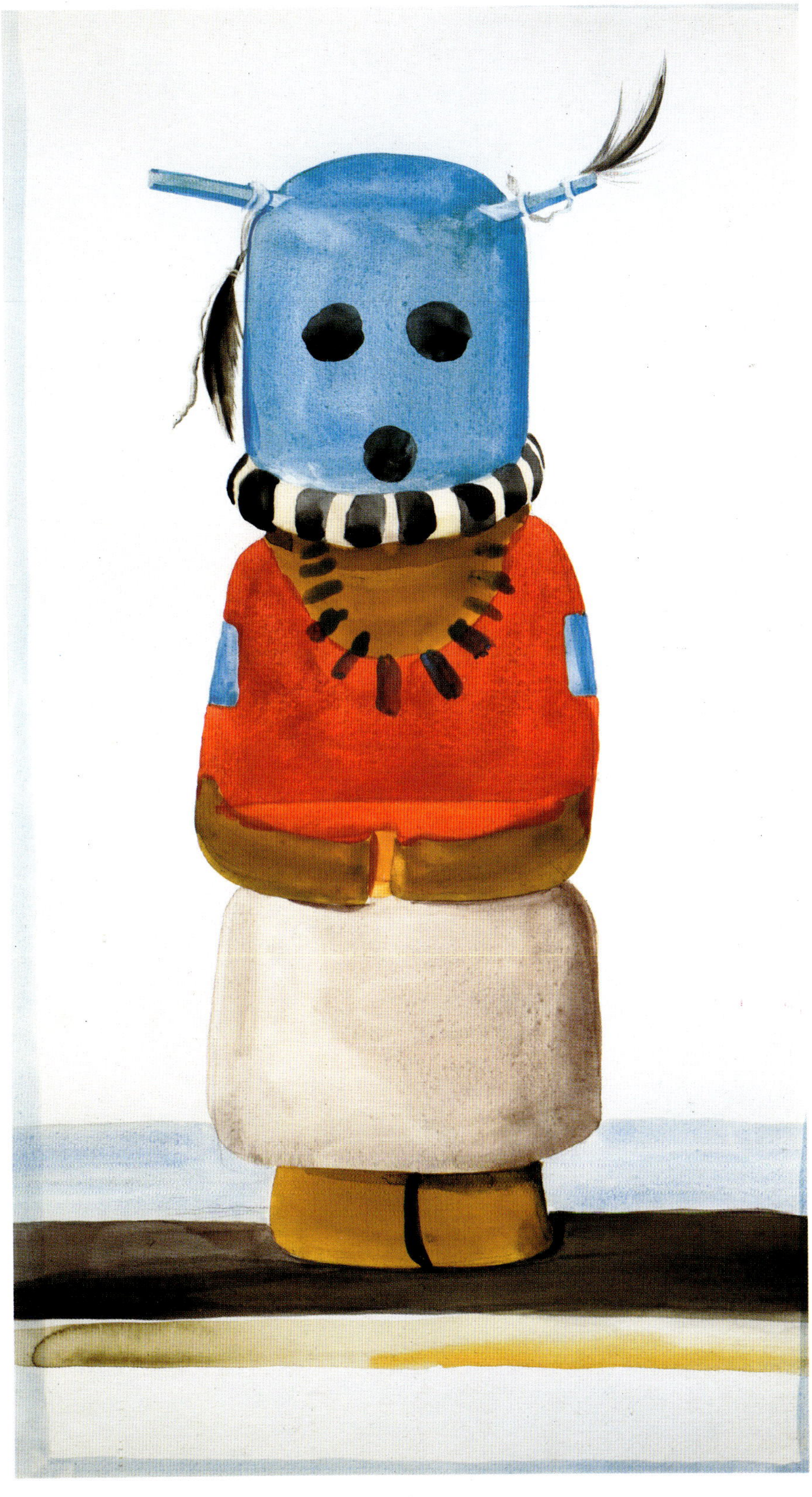

Plate 32. *Narcissa's Last Orchid*, 1941, pastel, 21 x 27 inches, Art Museum, Princeton University, Gift of David H. McAlpin

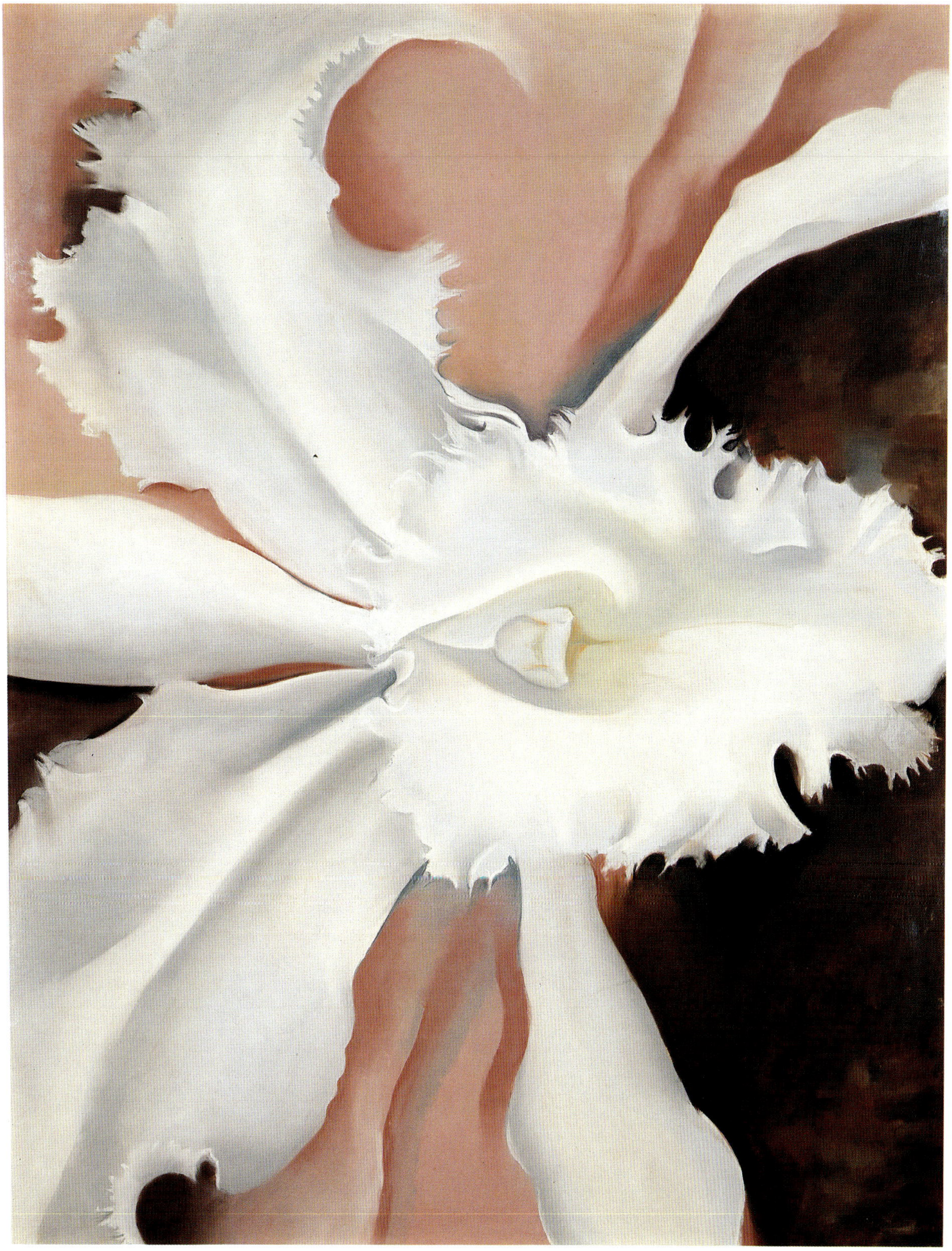

Plate 33. *Untitled 3* (formerly *My Heart*), 1944, pastel, 27-1/2 x 21-1/2 inches, The Museum, Texas Tech University, Gift of Helen DeVitt Jones to the West Texas Museum Association Collection

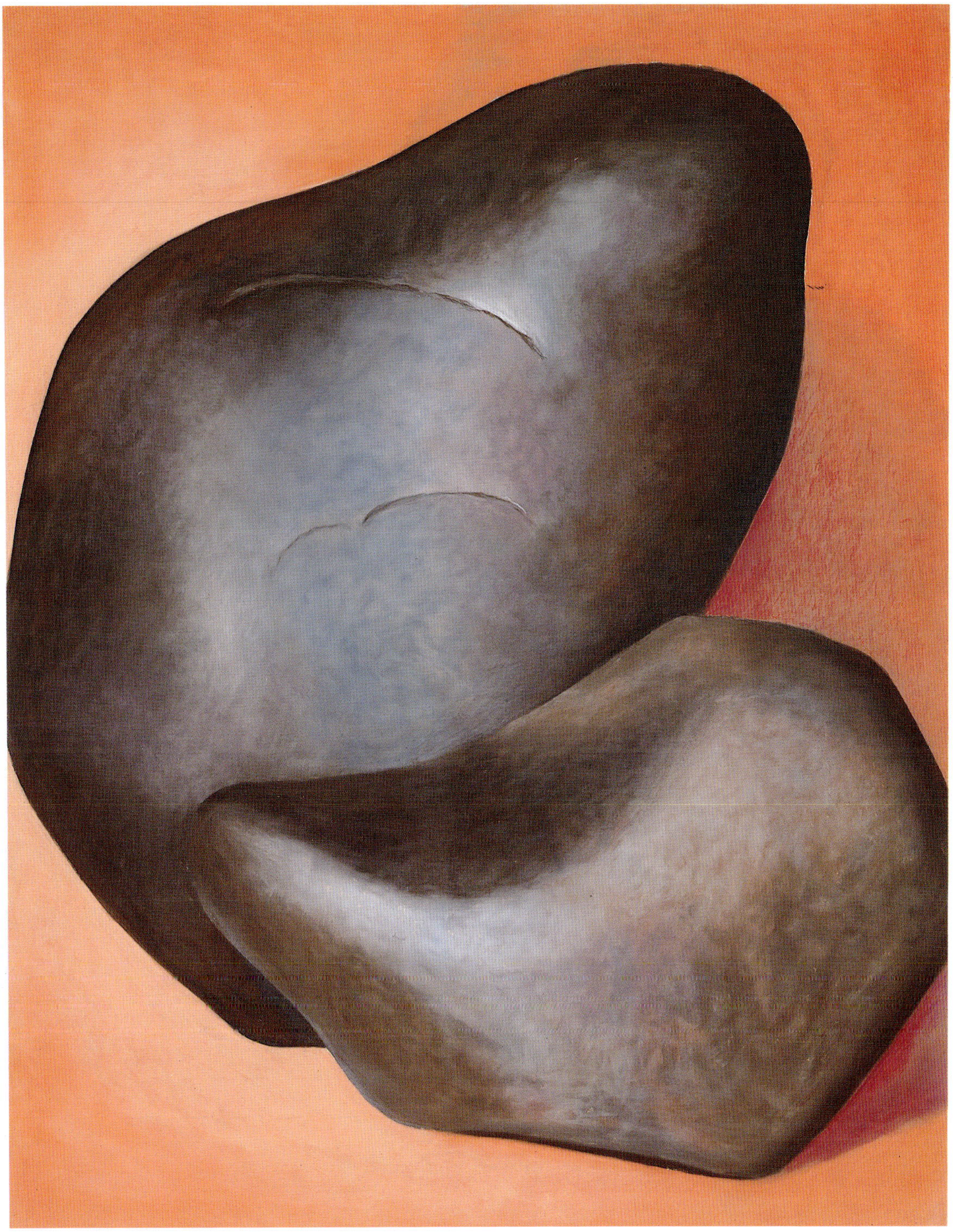

Plate 34. *Goat's Horn with Red*, 1945, pastel, 31-11/16 x 27-7/8 inches, Hirshhorn Museum and Sculpture Garden, Smithsonian Institution

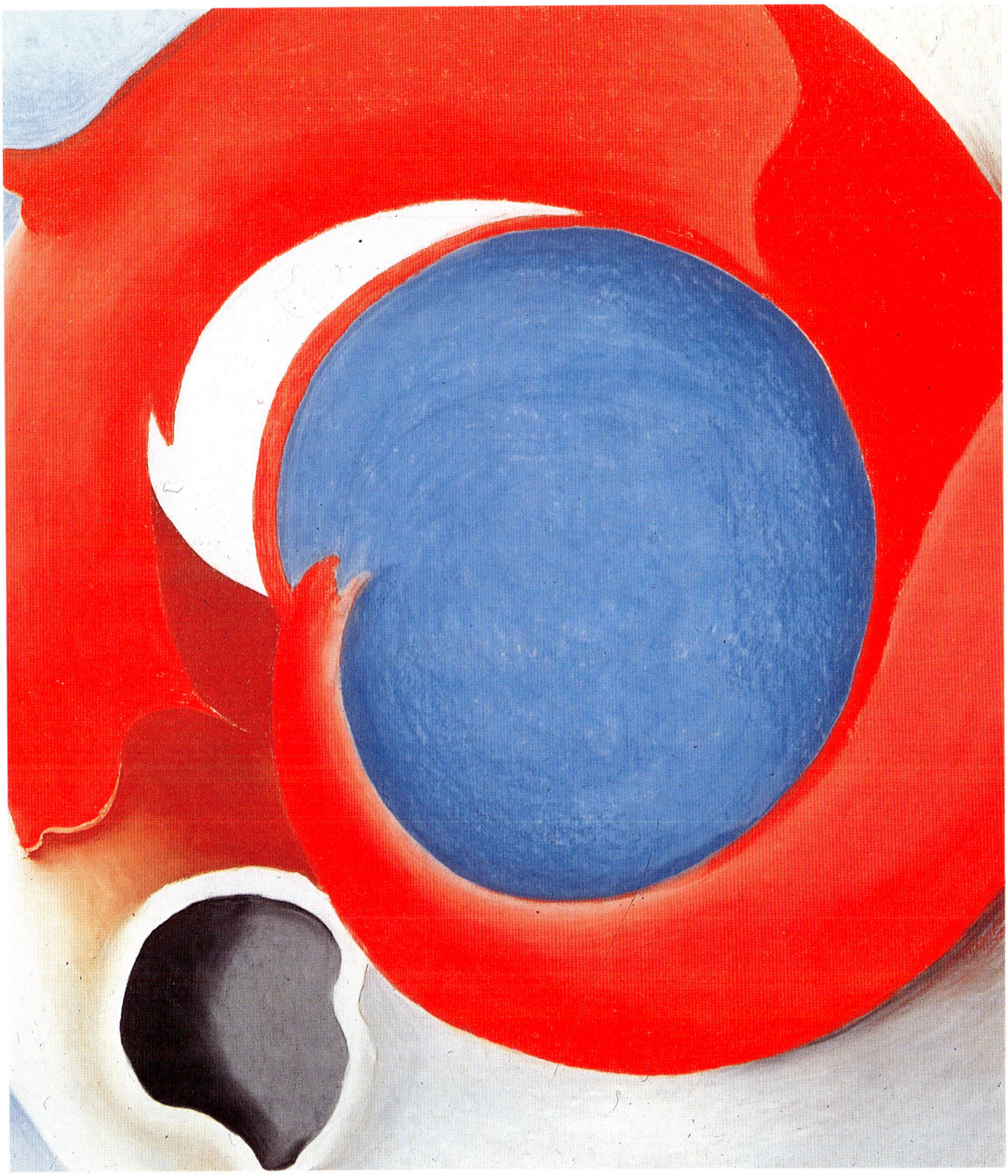

Plate 35. *Antelope Horns*, 1954, pencil, 19 x 24 inches, Anonymous loan

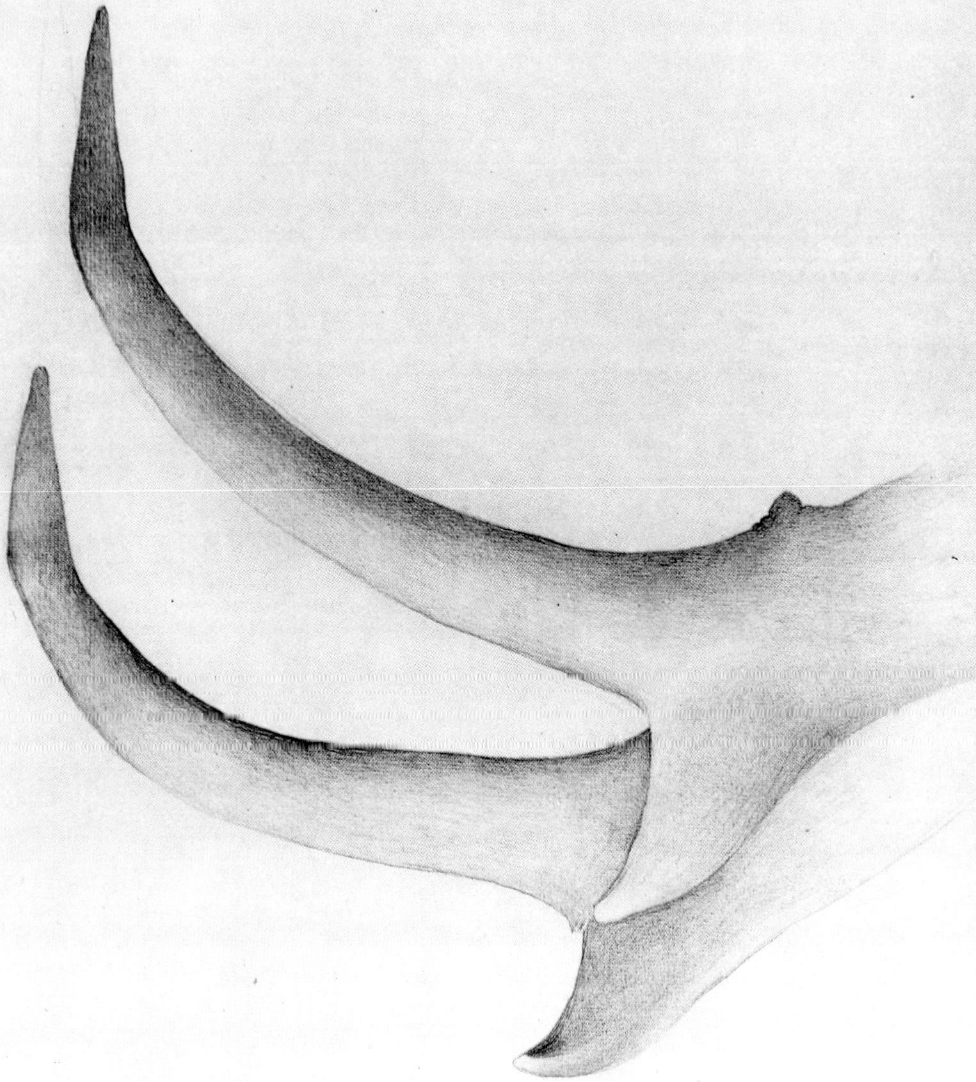

Plate 36. *Drawing* IV, 1959, charcoal, 18-1/2 x 24-1/2 inches, Whitney Museum of American Art, Gift of Chauncey L. Waddell, in honor of John I. H. Baur

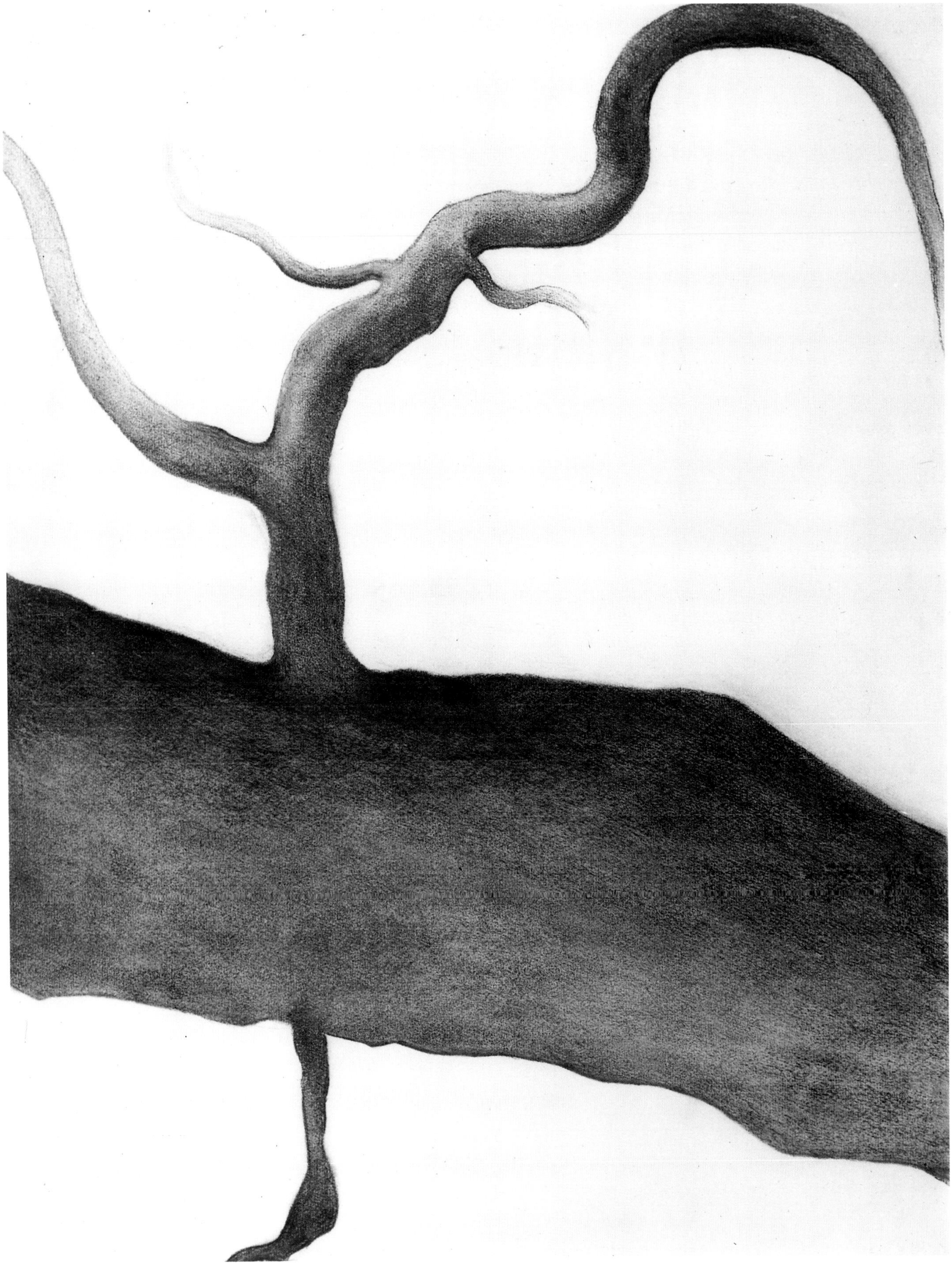

Plate 37. *Red Line with Circle*, 1977, watercolor, 29-1/2 x 22 inches, Anonymous loan through the Madison Art Center, Madison, Wisconsin

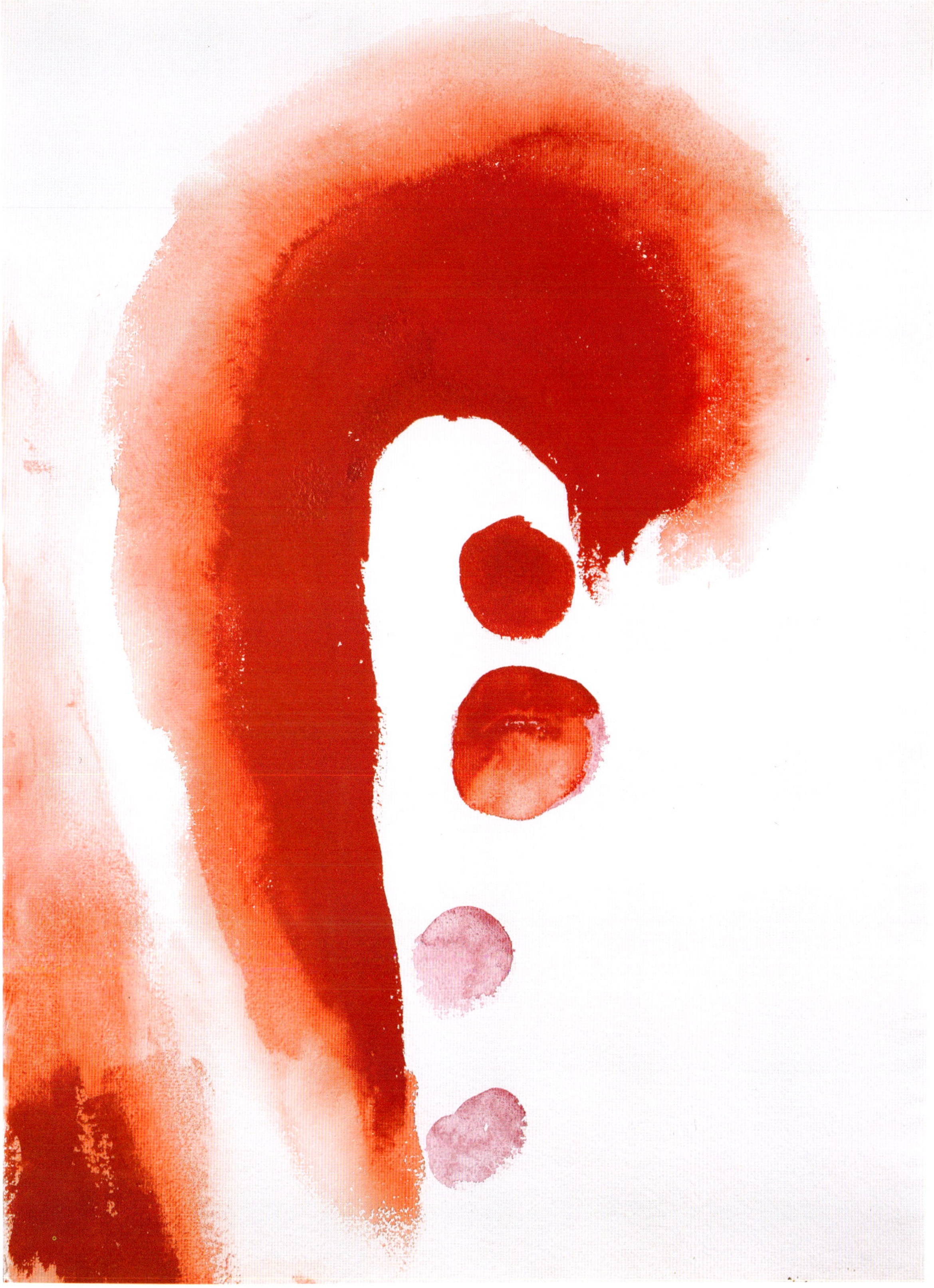

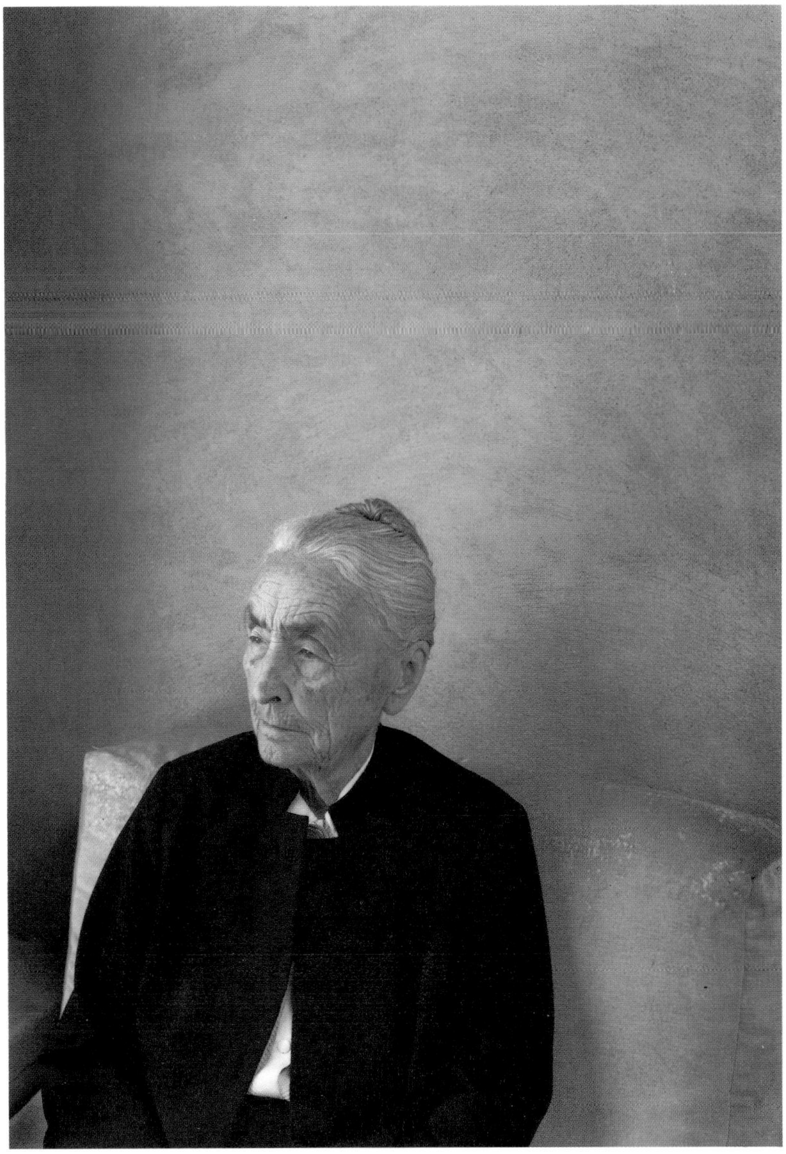

Georgia O'Keeffe in Abiquiu, New Mexico. Photograph by William Clift. © 1981. Collection of Museum of Fine Arts, Museum of New Mexico.

CHRONOLOGY

1887–1905 Born November 15 near Sun Prairie, Wisconsin, to Ida (Toto) and Francis O'Keeffe, the second of seven children. Raised on family's 600-acre farm and attended local elementary school and high schools in Madison, Wisconsin, and Chatham, Virginia. Had weekly private drawing lessons at ages of eleven and twelve.

1905–1906 Attended the School of the Art Institute of Chicago and studied with John Vanderpoel.

1907–1908 Attended Art Students League, New York, and visited Alfred Stieglitz' Little Galleries of the Photo Secession (later known as 291).

1908–1910 Temporarily abandoned fine art studies and worked as freelance commercial artist in Chicago.

1911–1913 Taught art in high school in Chatham, Virginia, and attended drawing classes at University of Virginia, Charlottesville. Became Art Supervisor in Amarillo Public Schools, Texas, August, 1912—Spring, 1914. During the summers of 1913–16, taught art at University of Virginia.

1914–1915 Attended Teacher's College, Columbia University, New York, to study with Arthur W. Dow. Became friend of Anita Pollitzer and began sending her drawings for critique in summer, 1915. Fall, 1915–March, 1916 taught art at Columbia College in Columbia, South Carolina. Did series of abstract charcoal drawings.

1916 In February returned to Teachers College for spring semester. May 23–July 5 had first public exhibition of her drawings and watercolors at 291 in a group show with Charles Duncan and Rene Lafferty. First meeting between O'Keeffe and Stieglitz. During summer taught at the University of Virginia. November–December was in group show organized by Stieglitz with Marsden Hartley, John Marin, Stanton Macdonald-Wright, and Abraham Walkowitz. September–February, 1918, taught art at West Texas State Normal College in Canyon, Texas, and worked actively in watercolor.

1917 April 3–May 14 had first one-person exhibition at 291. Traveled to New York during the summer to see show that Stieglitz rehung for her. Stieglitz made first photographs of O'Keeffe. Completed

Evening Star series while in Texas.

1918 February–May lived in Waring and San Antonio, Texas. Moved to New York in early summer, and in fall began series of annual vacations to Lake George, New York, with Stieglitz.

1918–1928 Lived and painted in New York and Lake George, with several trips to Maine.

1923 Stieglitz arranged for a show of one hundred works by O'Keeffe at Anderson Galleries, New York.

1924 Had joint exhibition with Stieglitz at Anderson Galleries. December 11, O'Keeffe and Stieglitz married.

1925 Work included in "Seven Americans" show at Anderson Galleries. O'Keeffe made first paintings of New York City buildings. In December Stieglitz opened the Intimate Gallery.

1926–1929 Annual exhibitions of new work at Stieglitz' Intimate Gallery.

1927 During the summer exhibited at the Brooklyn Museum.

1929 April–August took first trip to New Mexico with Rebecca Strand, as a guest of Mabel Dodge Luhan in Taos. Continued to travel to New Mexico almost every summer. Stieglitz closed The Intimate Gallery in June and opened An American Place in December with funds raised by Paul Strand and Dorothy Norman. In December five of her paintings were shown in the group show, "Paintings by Nineteen Living Americans," the second exhibition at the newly opened Museum of Modern Art.

1930 In February Stieglitz exhibited O'Keeffe's New Mexican works at An American Place, where she had annual exhibitions until 1946. June–September O'Keeffe stayed in Taos, New Mexico, with the Luhans. Before leaving she shipped a barrel of bones and fabric flowers east so she could continue painting New Mexican themes.

1931 April–July rented cottage on H & M Ranch in Alcalde, New Mexico.

1932 Drove through Gaspe area of Canada with Stieglitz' niece.

1933 Suffered physical collapse and recuperated in New York, Bermuda, and Lake George.

1934 First visit to Ghost Ranch, near Abiquiu, New Mexico, after three-year absence from New Mexico. Returned during summers.

1937 O'Keeffe stayed at Rancho de los Burros, near Ghost Ranch, New Mexico. Toured Indian country in western New Mexico, Arizona, and Colorado.

1938 *Life* magazine published photographic essay on O'Keeffe. Received honorary doctor of Fine Arts from College of William and Mary in Williamsburg, Virginia.

1939 Painted in Hawaii and selected as one of twelve most outstanding women for the past fifty years by the New York World's Fair Tomorrow Committee.

1940 Bought house and eight acres of land at Rancho de los Burros, New Mexico.

1943 January–February had first large retrospective exhibition at Art Institute of Chicago.

1946 Bought second home on three acres of land in Abiquiu, New Mexico, about sixteen miles from Ghost Ranch. May–August had retrospective exhibition at Museum of Modern Art, New York. July 13, Stieglitz died.

1947–1949 Spent time in New York settling Stieglitz' estate and preparing exhibitions of Stieglitz' collections at Museum of Modern Art and Art Institute of Chicago. Moved to New Mexico in 1949 and began living in Abiquiu house during winter and spring and at Rancho de los Burros during summer and autumn.

1950 One-person show at An American Place, which closed in November. Edith Gregor Halpert of the Downtown Gallery, New York, became dealer.

1952 Exhibited pastels from 1914-45 at Downtown Gallery, February–March.

1953 First trip to Europe (France and Spain).

1956 Traveled to Peru.

1959 Took a three-and-a-half-month trip around the world. Painted first cloud pictures.

1960 Retrospective exhibition at Worcester Art Museum, Worcester, Massachusetts.

1961 First of several raft trips down Colorado River.

1963 Ended her association with the Downtown Gallery; Doris Bry became her agent (until 1977). Traveled to Greece, Egypt, and Near East.

1966 Retrospective exhibition held at Amon Carter Museum of Western Art, Fort Worth, Texas, which traveled to Museum of Fine Arts, Houston, Texas, and Art Museum, University of New Mexico, Albuquerque.

1967 Traveled to England and Austin, Texas.

1969 Second rafting trip down Colorado River, repeated the next year.

1970 Retrospective exhibition held at Whitney Museum of American Art, New York, which traveled to Art Institute of Chicago and San Francisco Museum of Art.

1971 Lost central vision late in year, keeping only peripheral sight. Stopped painting.

1972 Met potter, Juan Hamilton, who taught her how to make hand-rolled pots. He became her assistant and encouraged her to paint again in watercolor and oil.

1974 *Some Memories of Drawings*, a portfolio of drawings with short texts written by the artist, was published by Atlantis Editions.

1975 Perry Miller Adato produced hour-long film on O'Keeffe and her work.

1975 Exhibited twelve paintings at inaugural exhibition of the Governor's Gallery, Santa Fe.

1976 *Georgia O'Keeffe*, with text by the artist, published by The Viking Press.

1977 O'Keeffe began working again in watercolor.

1978 Exhibition of photographs, "Georgia O'Keeffe: A Portrait by Alfred Stieglitz," was exhibited at Metropolitan Museum of Art, New York.

1979 Awarded the Medal of Freedom, the nation's highest civilian honor, by President Gerald Ford.

1982 Exhibited five paintings at the dedication of the New Wing of the Museum of Fine Arts, Santa Fe.

1984 Moved to Santa Fe, New Mexico.

1986 Died on March 6 at St. Vincent Hospital, Santa Fe.

1997 Opening of the Georgia O'Keeffe Museum in Santa Fe.

LIST OF ILLUSTRATIONS

All dimensions are in inches. Height precedes width. Asterisks denote inclusion in the exhibition at the Museum of Fine Arts, Museum of New Mexico.

Figure 1.
Black Lines, 1916
watercolor, 25 x 19
Courtesy of Andrew Crispo Gallery

Figure 2.
Roof with Snow, 1917
watercolor, 9 x 12
Amarillo Art Center

Figure 3.
Pink and Green Mountain, No. III, 1917
watercolor, 8-7/8 x 11-7/8
Milwaukee Art Museum, Gift of Mrs. Harry Lynde Bradley

Figure 4.
Train Coming In—Canyon, Texas, ca. 1918
watercolor, 12 x 9
Amarillo Art Center

Figure 5.
Blue #1, 1916
watercolor, 16 x 11
The Brooklyn Museum, Bequest of Mary T. Cockcroft

Figure 6.
Blue #2, 1916
watercolor, 15-7/8 x 10-15/16
The Brooklyn Museum, Bequest of Mary T. Cockcroft

Figure 7.
Blue #3, 1916
watercolor, 15-15/16 x 10-15/16
The Brooklyn Museum, Bequest of Mary T. Cockcroft

Figure 8.
Shell No. 1, 1932
pastel, 9-3/4 x 14-3/4
Courtesy of Hirschl and Adler Galleries, Inc., New York

Figure 9.
Banana Flower No. 1, 1933
charcoal, 22 x 15
The Arkansas Arts Center Foundation Collection

Figure 10.
Roses, 1934
pastel, 17-1/2 x 12
Beinecke Rare Book and Manuscript Library, Yale University

Figure 11.
Lightning at Sea, 1922
pastel, 19 x 25-1/2
The Lane Collection

* Plate 1.
Lady with Red Hair, ca. 1910
linoleum block print, 7-1/2 x 7
Courtesy of Gerald Peters Gallery, Santa Fe

* Plate 2.
Untitled Portrait, before 1917
monotype, 4 x 3
Anonymous loan

* Plate 3.
Still Life, before 1915
watercolor, 20-1/4 x 14-1/8
Elvehjem Museum of Art, University of Wisconsin-Madison,
Gift of Hermine Sauthoff Davidson
(Misspelling of O'KEEFE in lower right of watercolor may be explained by an early teacher's signing of O'Keeffe's student work. It is also possible that the person to whom O'Keeffe gave the watercolor wrote the name incorrectly on the surface as identification.)

* Plate 4.
Tent Door at Night, ca. 1913
watercolor, 18-15/16 x 24-3/4
University Art Museum, University of New Mexico, Albuquerque

* Plate 5.
Train at Night in the Desert, 1916
charcoal, 24-3/4 x 19-1/4
Anonymous loan

Plate 6.
Train at Night in the Desert, 1916
watercolor, 12 x 8-7/8
The Museum of Modern Art, New York. Acquired with matching funds from the Committee on Drawing and the National Endowment for the Arts.

Plate 7.
Blue #4, 1916
watercolor, 15-7/8 x 10-15/16
The Brooklyn Museum, Bequest of Mary T. Cockcroft

* Plate 8.
Blue I, ca. 1917
watercolor, 30-3/4 x 22-3/8
Collection of Robert L. B. Tobin

* Plate 9.
Abstraction, 1917
watercolor, 15-3/4 x 10-7/8
Collection of Mr. and Mrs. Gerald P. Peters

* Plate 10.
Red, Blue, and Green, ca. 1916
watercolor, 17-1/2 x 13
Courtesy of Washburn Gallery, New York

* Plate 11.
Blue Hill #2, ca. 1916
watercolor, 8-3/4 x 11-3/4
Anonymous loan through the Columbus Museum of Art, Ohio

* Plate 12.
Pink and Green Mountain, No. 1, 1917
watercolor, 8-7/8 x 11-7/8
The Helen Foresman Spencer Museum of Art,
Museum Purchase: Letha Churchill Walker Fund

* Plate 13.
Landscape and Layered Mountain, 1917
watercolor, 8-7/8 x 12
Collection of Mr. and Mrs. Warren Adelson

* Plate 14.
Portrait W, No. 1, 1917
watercolor, 9 x 12
Courtesy of Sid Deutsch Gallery, New York

* Plate 15.
Seated Nude X1, 1917
watercolor, 11-7/8 x 8-7/8
The Metropolitan Museum of Art, Purchase, Mr. and Mrs. Milton Petrie Gift, 1981

* Plate 16.
Trees, 1917
watercolor, 19 x 14-1/2
Collection of Mark Carliner

* Plate 17.
The Flag, 1918
watercolor, 11-7/8 x 8-3/4
Milwaukee Art Museum, Gift of Mrs. Harry Lynde Bradley

* Plate 18.
Evening Star No. II, 1917
watercolor, 9 x 12
Anonymous loan

Plate 19.
Evening Star No. III, 1917
watercolor, 9 x 12
The Museum of Modern Art, Mr. and Mrs. Donald B. Straus Fund

* Plate 20.
Evening Star No. V, 1917
watercolor, 9 x 12
Anonymous loan

* Plate 21.
Evening Star No. VII, 1917
watercolor, 9 x 12
Collection of Dore Previn

* Plate 22.
Evening Star, 1917
watercolor, 13-3/4 x 17-3/4
Yale University Art Gallery, The John Hill Morgan, B.A. 1893, Fund, the Leonard C. Hanna, Jr. B.A. 1913 Fund and Gifts of friends in honor of Theodore E. Stebbins, Jr. B.A. 1960

* Plate 23.
Canna Lily, 1919
watercolor, 23 x 12-7/8
Columbus Museum of Art, Museum Purchase: Derby Fund

Plate 24.
Red Canna, ca. 1920
watercolor, 19-5/16 x 13
Yale University Art Gallery, Gift of George Hopper Fitch, B.A. 1932, and Mrs. Fitch

Plate 25.
Lake George and Woods, ca. 1922
pastel, 16 x 13-3/4
Collection of Mr. and Mrs. John Palmer Leeper

* Plate 26.
Maine, 1922
watercolor, 18 x 11
Courtesy of Kennedy Galleries, New York

* Plate 27.
New York Rooftops, ca. 1925–30
charcoal, 24-1/2 x 18-3/4
The Fine Arts Museums of San Francisco, Achenbach Foundation for Graphic Arts, Gift of Mrs. Charlotte S. Mack

* Plate 28.
East River with Sun, 1926
pastel, 10-7/8 x 27-7/8
Anonymous loan

* Plate 29.
Shell, ca. 1928
charcoal, 18-11/16 x 24-3/4
National Gallery of Art, Gift of Dorothy Edinburg

* Plate 30.
Banyon Tree Trunk, Bermuda, 1934
pencil, 21-3/4 x 14-3/4
Courtesy of Hirschl and Adler Galleries, Inc., New York

* Plate 31.
Blue-Headed Indian Doll, 1935
watercolor, 20-1/2 x 11-1/2
Collection of King Investments Co., Dallas, Texas

Plate 32.
Narcissa's Last Orchid, 1941
pastel, 21 x 27
Art Museum, Princeton University, Gift of David H. McAlpin

* Plate 33.
Untitled 3 (formerly *My Heart*), 1944
pastel, 27-1/2 x 21-1/2
The Museum, Texas Tech University, Gift of Helen DeVitt Jones to the West Texas Museum Association Collection

Plate 34.
Goat's Horn with Red, 1945
pastel, 31-11/16 x 27-7/8
Hirshhorn Museum and Sculpture Garden, Smithsonian Institution

* Plate 35.
Antelope Horns, 1954
pencil, 19 x 24
Anonymous loan

* Plate 36.
Drawing IV, 1959
charcoal, 18-1/2 x 24-1/2
Whitney Museum of American Art, Gift of Chauncey L. Waddell in honor of John I. H. Baur

* Plate 37.
Red Line with Circle, 1977
watercolor, 29-1/2 x 22
Anonymous loan through the Madison Art Center, Madison, Wisconsin

LENDERS TO THE EXHIBITION

Mr. and Mrs. Warren Adelson, New York

Mark Carliner, Studio City, California

Columbus Museum of Art, Columbus, Ohio

Sid Deutsch Gallery, New York

Elvehjem Museum of Art, University of Wisconsin, Madison, Wisconsin

The Fine Arts Museums of San Francisco, Achenbach Foundation for Graphic Arts, San Francisco, California

Hirschl and Adler Galleries, Inc., New York

Kennedy Galleries, New York

King Investments Co., Dallas, Texas

The Metropolitan Museum of Art, New York

Milwaukee Art Museum, Milwaukee, Wisconsin

The Museum, Texas Tech University, Lubbock, Texas

National Gallery of Art, Washington, D.C.

Mr. and Mrs. Gerald Peters, Santa Fe, New Mexico

Gerald Peters Gallery, Santa Fe, New Mexico

Dore Previn, Los Angeles, California

The Helen Foresman Spencer Museum of Art, University of Kansas, Lawrence, Kansas

Robert L. B. Tobin, San Antonio, Texas

University Art Museum, University of New Mexico, Albuquerque, New Mexico

Washburn Gallery, New York

Whitney Museum of American Art, New York

Yale University Art Gallery, New Haven, Connecticut

Anonymous collectors